GUIDE
MENOR

Es Caixer Fadrí

© **Triangle Postals SL**
Sant Lluís, Menorca
Tel. +34 971 15 04 51
www.triangle.cat

Text
Joan Montserrat

Photographs
Jaume Serrat: Pages: 4; 5; 6; 8; 9; 12; 13; 18 (2); 19; 20 (1); 26;
27; 29; 31 (1); 32-33; 34 (1-2-4); 38; 39; 43; 47; 48 (1); 50 (1);
50-51; 54 (1); 56 (1); 56-57; 58 (1); 58-59; 60 (1); 60-61; 64;
65; 66-67; 68 (1); 68-69; 70-71; 72 (1); 74 (1); 74-75; 78 (1); 80
(1); 91; 98; 103; 104; 115; 116; 119; 121 (1); 122 (1); 123; 124
(1); 124-125; 126; 129; 132; 135; 136; 138 (2); 140 (1); 140-
141; 147; 148; 152; 153; 154; 155; 157; 160; 162; 163; 166;
167; 168-169; 170 (2); 172; 174; 175; 179; 198; 199; 201; 202;
205 (1); 206; 207; 208; 209; 212; 215 (1); 217; 219 (1,2); 220;
223 (2); 241. **Lluís Bertran:** 15; 21; 23; 62 (1); 88 (1); 180-181;
183; 185; 186; 189; 190-191; 197; 205 (2); 224; 225; 226; 232;
233; 235. **Carmen Vila:** 42; 66; 76-77; 78-79; 80-81; 101; 122
(2); 136 (1); 149; 165; 194; 195; 210 (4); 219 (3); 228; 255 (2).
Juanjo Pons: 2; 31 (2); 48-49; 52 (1); 52-53; 54-55; 72-73; 76 (1);
82 (1); 82-83; 84 (1); 96; 106; 138 (1); 158-159; 210 (1). **Ricard
Pla:** 20 (2); 22; 84-85; 87; 88-89; 93; 119 (2); 120 (1); 130; 137;
170 (1); 171; 188; 211; 255 (1). **Museu de Menorca:** 1; 14; 17;
108; 109; 110; 111. **Biel Calafat:** 89 (1); 95; 97; 128; 131; 223
(1), 231. **Francis Abbot:** 36 (2); 62-63; 70(1); 215 (2). **Melba
Levick:** flap 2; 18 (1); 24-25; 230. **Jordi Puig:** flap 1; 36 (1); 210
(2-3). **Xavi Carreras:** 94; 143; 151; 191. **J. Escandell:** 120-121.
Ecomuseu de Cavalleria: 167 (1). **Oriol Alamany:** 10. **Miguel
Cao:** 34 (3). **Oriol Aleu:** 228, 229. **Kike Cardona:** 245. **Isolda
Delgado:** 36 (3-4). **Joan Mercadal:** 37; 44; 45; 107. **Laia
Moreno:** 2. **Iñaki Relanzón:** 35. **Carles Virgili:** 243.

Translation
Steve Cedar

Cartography
Montse Puig and Germán Campos

Design
Joan Colomer

Layout
Vador Minobis and Germán Campos

Printed in Barcelona, 05-2014

Registration number: B-3061-2010   ISBN: 978-84-8478-305-3

CONTENTS

Many houses conserve elements from other times for ornamental purposes

Menorcan myths of beauty and peace, captured in this image of Cala Pregonda

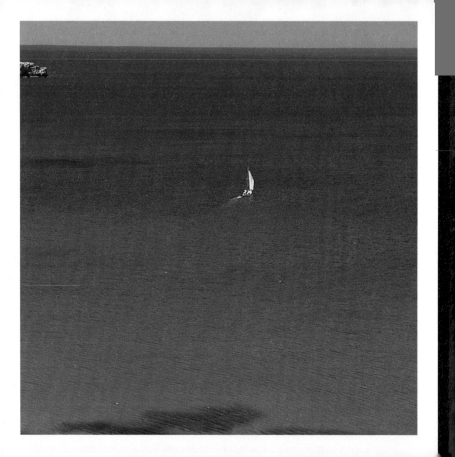

MENORCA

A SINGULAR ISLE

Those who know the four major islands of the Autonomous Region of the Balearic Islands often share the opinion that each one is very different. Later, if they have known them for some time, it is also quite common for them to add some comment about the changes caused by the massive development in tourism. Everything changes, but the globalisation to which they are subject does not mean that Mallorca has lost its ancestral essence or Eivissa its African warmth, or Formentera the Edenic charm of small and faraway places… and **Menorca** can provide us with a little of the above and many more peculiarities that make it even more distinct, if one might say so.

Today it could be seen as a loose leaf of the European continent, but very sensibly anchored in the heart of the westernmost part of the Mediterranean. Its 700 km², spread over eight districts, offer a great deal indeed. This is something inevitably discovered by simply abandoning the automatic sun-worshipping, which is common and almost obligatory during the summer months. This use of holiday time is fully justified by the quality of Menorca's beaches and coves but, even more so than other destinations, here the "everything else" that usually forms part of traditional holiday brochures is interesting and gratifying. The artisans' markets, the festivals, the prehistoric monuments, the local gastronomic products, the footprints of history on each street corner… all invite us to calmly enjoy —this is one of the abilities often attributed to the Menorcan people— a spot that could become a model to follow if the objectives of sustainable growth currently proposed are achieved.

The island has crossed the barrier of ninety thousand inhabitants, something that would have been unimaginable fifty years ago, but it is clearly still a long way off from suffering the nightmare caused by demographic growth. Although visitors increase the number by almost double during the high season, the share of countryside is still very high and enjoying nature can be extended to the domains of the sea.

It is difficult to take in the entire coastline by land due to the layout of the roads, so leisure boating is therefore the alternative. That is why there is an increasing popularity to copy the local craze for doing a tour of the island by the *Cami de cavalls* or on family-style boats. There are also many deep-sea divers, since the beauty of the seabed goes perfectly with the coastline.

Also on the increase are the number of people attracted by the recently inaugurated rural tourism establishments, experiencing directly a practically unharmed natural environment (agriculture has been the key in its upkeep until now), along with the curiosity to discover aspects of island life that were previously hidden on the supposition that they were of no interest to anyone. Everything changes then, as we mentioned before. Luck may have it that these changes are occurring with a very clear view of the risks that abuse of the environment entails. It is no surprise, therefore, that the warm welcome given to the stranger also brings with it a special plea: to respect this environment in the same way that the local population has done so until now.

Beautiful coves, quiet moments: the island's greatest tourist attraction

The herds of cows still form part of the rural landscape

ARCHAEOLOGY

The presence of many prehistoric monuments in the surrounding countryside generally surprises the new visitor. But contact with something that belongs to both the present and the distant past very soon enthrals whoever approaches and examines them. Time is needed to see all the excavations catalogued, but it is easy and highly advisable to see the main ones, since the skills of the ancient dwellers in the constructive use of stone are quite fascinating. The majority are well signposted and will be commented on in the following pages.

Experts locate the earliest remains at around 2500 BC (see table next page), but the most outstanding series corresponds to the **Talayotic** period. The settlements of that time lasted beyond the Roman colonisation, reached the Middle Ages and were even used to provide shelter for livestock in relatively recent times.

The area around the *taula* of Torralba d'en Salord is one of the most stunning

It is the prehistorically dated monuments where the uniqueness of some elements really stands out. They are the **talayots**, or tower-like monuments, located in the highest point of the settlements and seem to provide an improvement in the need for constant vigilance. In reality, they hide small funeral chambers. The small *navetes*, so-called as they appear to be inverted ship hulls, were used as sepulchres and ossuaries. Finally there are the *taules*, flat stones, which it is believed were connected to Tauric rites and that their simple layout, a crudely sculpted transversal block over another sunken into the ground —a simple *taula* or table— are among the most spectacular.

Other monuments from bygone times have also survived until today, such as the Paleochristian basilicas of North African influence (Vandal reign of Carthage) and of Byzantine influence (Roman Empire of the Orient). There are remains of these in **Son Bou**, **Illa del Rei**, **Es Fornàs**, **Cap des Port de Fornells** and **Illa d'en Colom**.

	Periods	Dwellings	Burials
2500-1800 B.C.	Chalcolitich- Early Bronze Pre-talayotic I	Huts of stones and branches, adaptation of caves, first settlements and burial chambers	Megalithic sepulchres or Hypogeums (burial chambers)
1800-1500 B.C.	Early Bronze Pre-talayotic II	Huts of stones and branches, adaptation of caves, first settlements and burial chambers	Chambers of an intermediate type
1500-1000 B.C.	Middle and Late Bronze	Talayots or towers, *taules* or stone tables, *taula* areas and circular dwellings	Elongated chambers

Taula of Torre Trencada

A bucolic scene in the town of Talatí de Dalt

The port of Maó in the mid-19th century (oil painting by Joan Font i Vidal)

HISTORY AND SOCIETY

Menorca shares with the neighbouring islands a relationship with all the seafaring peoples of the ancient Mediterranean, occupation of the Muslim civilisation, dominant in Spain until the time of the Catholic Monarchs (15th century), and the conquest and later colonisation by the Catalan-Aragonese Crown. Even then, however, there was a certain independent spirit, and the special circumstances experienced during the 18th century had a big impact on this development, providing the island with its own differentiating traits that would consign it with a secondary role that has, on occasions, been given to it.

When the British saw their presence confirmed by the Treaty of Utrecht (1713), they had already been using the Port of Maó as one of their main bases in the Mediterranean for almost fifty years. In fact, the changes of nationality in the 18th century (the British, French and Spanish alternated in governing the island) ended up representing a substantial improvement after the troubled experiences of the 16th and 17th centuries. Years of obscurantism and uncertainty, with internal conflicts and constant attacks from outside led by pirates of all sorts, was later followed by epidemics and famines that decimated the population.

It has sometimes been said that if the stamp of successive occupiers on the island has lasted more than at other latitudes, this is due to the more or less pacific adaptation to foreign ways. There still remain place names of Arab origin —*rafal* or *bini*, for example, often appear—, or vocabulary and phrases that come from English. It is, however, the maintenance of a non-exclusive identity, to which it returned —according to the level of repression— after each seizure of sovereignty, that has given Menorca its strength against any inter-

CHRONOLOGY

Circa 2500 BC
First megalithic constructions (the island was already inhabited in the Neolithic period and even before).

Circa 1300 BC
Transition from a pre-Talayotic culture (*Naveta* des Tudons) to the Talayotic period itself.

Circa 500 BC
First contacts made with the Punic world. In 205 BC General Mago gave his name to the enclave that is today Maó.

123 BC
Quintus Cecilius Metellus annexes Menorca to the Roman Empire.

417
Conversions in the Maó Jewish colony organised by Bishop Severo.

425
Vandal invasion.

534
Dominion of the Byzantine Empire.

707
First contacts made with the Islamic world.

902
Incorporation into the Cordoba Caliphate.

1015
The island comes to depend on the Taifa kingdom of Dènia.

1108
Incursion of Norman troops of King Sigurd.

1116
The Almoravides provide a period of growth and peace until the arrival of the Almohades (1203).

1287
Alfons III conquers Menorca for the Catalan-Aragonese Crown and undertakes its colonisation.

1301
Under the reign of Jaume II the island achieves its own legal and administrative system.

1348
The epidemic of the plague that devastates Europe reaches the island.

1410
Internal struggles. The rural population confronts the urban dwellers and Maó (together with Alaior and Es Mercadal) against Ciutadella.

1463
Menorca rises up and supports Catalonia against Joan II of Mallorca. Ciutadella lines up with the King and a situation of civil war ensues.

1535
Barbarossa pillages Maó as reprisal for the defeat of Tunis against the imperial armies.

ference. Made weak by its own insularity, it nevertheless has an extra power of resistance against setbacks. In the past, it was the submission of a highly stratified society to self-governed institutions that enabled it to maintain its cohesion. It should also be mentioned that since its introduction, the use of the Catalan language has never been lost. Catalan is today the official and most commonly used language in the whole Balearic Islands region and is a common link of unity and identity (although the changes in phonetics and lexicon mark differences between the islands and even between one district and another). Returning to that outlined above, the co-existence between troops and civilians of different languages, and even religions during the 18th century was of a very special nature because it had a positive effect on economic matters. It also signified entering into Europe, or the World, as it was seen in those times. Neither should we fool ourselves that these administrations solved all the problems of structural order, but they did change the course of history. Despite the return, with the absolutist Spanish administration, and despite the consequent loss of freedom and return to poverty, causing another of the distinct migratory processes —this time to Algiers and other North African cities—, the Menorcan people were not, and would not be, a silent or defeatist community.

In the countryside, the atmosphere of bygone times can still be sensed

16

When, in the mid-19th century, industrialisation allowed for relative recovery, the new productive methods and the creation of a workers' movement became the seeds for many changes in the social fabric. The 20th century opened with an authentically democratic and progressive mood, still fearful for the swings of fortune of the economy, but breathing airs of freedom that differed greatly from the tyrannical operations of other parts.

Perhaps it is for this reason that the Spanish Civil War had very dramatic repercussions on Menorcan society. These effects had an influence before, during and in a very extended aftermath, a post-war period that would last until 1977, when free elections, the first since the Second Republic, once again marked out the path for the Balearic community to recover their own governmental bodies differentiated by island.

1558
The Ottomans destroy Ciutadella and capture the majority of the population.

1570
Felipe II plans to evacuate the population and leave only a garrison on the island. The Menorcan people oppose this measure.

1627
Reform of the University General which forces Ciutadella to cede representation to the other towns.

1706
Carlist Menorcans confront soldiers of Philip in the outbreak of the Spanish War of Succession.

1708
British troops land in support of the Archduke Carlos.

1713
The Treaty of Utrecht consecrates the presence of the British on the island (end of the War of Succession).

1756
The French land in Ciutadella. Siege and taking of Castell Sant Felip. The troops sent by Richelieu will remain seven years on the island.

1763
The Treaty of Versalles returns Menorca to Great Britain. The "2nd occupation" begins.

1782
The Duke of Crillon conquers the island for Charles III of Spain.

1785
Blowing up of Castell de Sant Felip.

1798
New British landing, the "3rd occupation".

1802
The Treaty of Amiens orders the definitive devolution to Spain.

1820
Faced with the ban on importing cereals and pulses, the disaster of the island's economy causes heavy emigration.

1830
New migratory flow towards Algiers after the conquest of this area by the French.

1850
Installation of the first footwear factories in Ciutadella.

1860
Visit of Isabel II to the works of La Mola, begun in 1840.

1898
The loss of Cuba damages footwear exports.

1906
The year of hunger, *S'any de sa fam*, forces many Menorcans to emigrate due to unemployment.

1909
The Society to Attract Foreigners and Promote Excursions is founded, the predecessor of the Tourist Promotion Office.

1930
The world crisis of '29 also reaches Menorca. Strike by the footwear workers of Alaior.

1936
During the Civil War, Menorca remains loyal to the Republic.

1953
First charter flight from London.

1983
The *Consell Insular de Menorca* (Menorca Island Council) is formed.

1993
UNESCO awards Menorca with the title of Biosphere Reserve.

S'Homo des Be

Oil painting documenting the presence of the British fleet in Port de Maó

ARCHITECTURE

Architecture is a fairly faithful reflection of the evolution, growth or decline of a people. It can be a reliable, incorruptible witness, almost always irremovable, of their past behaviour and become the notary that records the day-to-day life without any significant omissions. In Menorca the houses and monuments enable us to "read" history, the passing and settlement of distinct peoples and cultures in the region: in visits to the prehistoric excavations or in strolls around the village streets, through the architecture one can take in detailed lessons of knowing how people live and survive.

Recent works use traditional materials to adapt them to the environment

Here there is also a very characteristic rural architecture, starting with the unending dry stone walls marking the property borders and protecting the crops from the wind. Within the great squares they outline, white houses are scattered amidst the green fields or form little bunches around the villages. They have greatly contributed to the typical images seen on posters with which the island has

In the countryside, homes grew according to their needs

Roofs and eaves ensure the channelling of rainwater to the deposits

The *porxada*, or porch, is a basic space in the country house

The façades of many rural houses were renovated in the late 19th century

Casa Mir, a Modernist building in Costa de ses Voltes in Maó

announced itself to the outside world. They are made of large blocks of *marès* (sandstone) and wild olive tree wood, the only building materials at hand in bygone times and which were usually found "on site". They have Arab tile roofing, as the first link of a collecting system that allowed the desired amount of rainwater to be stored in cisterns and deposits. They have ovens for cooking bread and large dining rooms for the day labourers. They are protected from the elements by small openings facing north and *porxades* (porches) facing south. They extend according to the expansion of tasks and needs of the families inhabiting them.

Menorcan country houses are a fine example of adapting to the environment, although one day they will need a certificate of authenticity. Their leading role as mankind's contribution to the landscape has increased with the recession experienced by the agricultural sector. Some of the more imposing ones are in the process of, or have already been transformed into very popular country hotels. There are estates, previously cultivated as farms, that have been converted into leisure complexes, up to the point

Imposing steps rise from the entrance courtyards

Additions in neo-classical style "enhance" some country houses

where the friendliness of the white cottages, with their "extensive garden" and suitably removed from pollution, has seduced a new population of urban origin which is gradually replacing their former inhabitants. The demand has forced purchasing prices up so much that there is now a high risk of "rural urbanisation", new complexes of artificial copies of the model.

Entrance of a stately home in Ciutadella, the Torre Saura palace

Barqueres in Alcalfar

BIOSPHERE RESERVE

SITES OF SPECIAL INTEREST
GEOGRAPHY AND CLIMATE
FLORA AND FAUNA
 SARGANTANES
 THE MENORCAN HORSE
 THE "RED" COWS
PARK OF S'ALBUFERA DES GRAU AND FAVÀRITX
ECOMUSEUM CAP DE CAVALLERIA

Typical scenery in the northern part of the island

BIOSPHERE RESERVE

In 1993 Menorca was declared a **Biosphere Reserve** by UNESCO as part of its Man and Biosphere programme. This declaration was a backing for those who defended a non-aggressive growth model towards the natural values and areas of rural landscape. The Law of Natural Spaces, stipulating different levels of protection for almost half of the region, also confirmed the institutions' commitment to being part of this ever-increasing environmental concern.

It is quite clear that conservationists' opinions must be taken into account in the organisation of the region and the urban planning programmes which, just like the supervision of activity in the tourism sector and the maintenance and promotion of the historical heritage, are responsibilities of the **Consell Insular de Menorca**, the local government body. With the **Biosphere Reserve** having completed twenty years, the balance is obviously positive in terms of maintaining the protected spaces and the opening and equipping of them for visits and pleasure. It is true that there are still totally divergent attempts of private and public actions, but an attitude shared by the vast majority of the people of Menorca has been achieved. This attitude is demonstrated, for example, in the growing recreational use of the **Camí de Cavalls**, the intensely reclaimed historic perimeter route, so that controlled access is possible in these areas and their environmental quality is not affected. Recovered and signposted, it is a space used for tourism by walkers, horse-riders and mountain bikers.

Regarding the events relating to the Biosphere reserve, this will soon have its own information centre, situated in the S'Enclusa mountain, close to Ferreries, and, in advance of the planned facilities, already operating is a documentation centre in Sa Granja, close to Maó (see www.biosferamenorca.org). Currently, when the Menorcan economy revolves inevitably around the tourist industry, we must hope that society keeps a cool head, as on other occasions, and knows how to administer its greatest wealth: environmental balance.

SITES OF SPECIAL INTEREST

1
North Coast of Ciutadella
2
La Vall
3
From Els Alocs
to Fornells
4
La Mola and the
Albufera de Fornells
5
Bella Vista
6
From Port d'Addaia
to S'Albufera des Grau
7
S'Albufera des Grau
(Central Area
and Natural Park)
8
From S'Albufera to
La Mola
8b
Sant Isidre-Binisermenya
9
From Cala Sant Esteve
to Caló de Rafalet
11
From Biniparratx
to Llucalcari
12
Son Bou and Barranc
de Sa Vall
13
From Binigaus
to Cala Mitjana
14
South Coast
of Ciutadella
15
Son Olivaret
16
Camí de baix
(Degollador)
17
Santa Àgueda-S'Enclusa
18
El Toro
19
Penyes d'Egipte

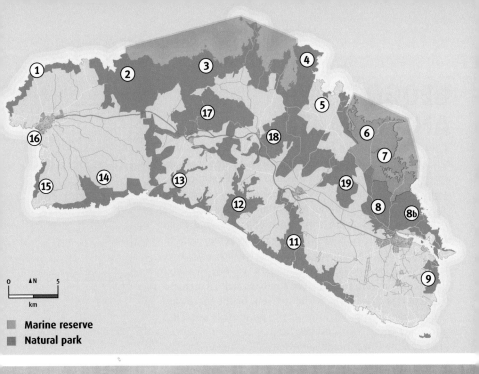

Bay of Fornells with El Toro in the background

GEOGRAPHY AND CLIMATE

If the cut outlined by the map of the Port of Maó were extended inland, Menorca would be divided into two very different islands; to the south, the area of the **Es migjorn**, or southerly wind, is made up of Miocene lands of a limestone composition, whereas in the **tramuntana**, to the north, the rocks are siliceous, with a presence of schists, clays and slates, providing the soils with a great chromatic variety. This part, older, has a gently undulating surface, with three outstanding high points: Santa Àgueda (264m), S'Enclusa (274m) and El Toro (358m). The southern strip, flatter and calcareous, is characterised, alternatively, by the succession of deep cuts inland, forming small ravines that open out onto white sandy coves and beaches.

The climate is warm and very humid if compared to the rest of the archipelago. For those who have only stayed in Menorca in summer, it is difficult to imagine the explosion of greens present throughout the rest of the year. With the exception of generalised drought years, the regular rainfall and abundance of winter dew compensates for the lack of rainfall in August. Furthermore, the island has a very particular relationship with the wind: the absence of natural obstacles exposes it to all its battering. The winds from the northern quadrant dominate, but the powerful *tramuntana* blows with more force and insistence, with speeds that range from 35 kph to over 90 kph. It has a stunning effect on the environment, the trees and shrubs taking on strange leaning formations, but it also guarantees a surplus of clear skies, a clean atmosphere and radiant sunshine. Extremely low temperatures are unknown and one needs to refer to the records to see when the last snowfall was. In summer, the average temperature is 25° and in winter 12°.

Average temperatures

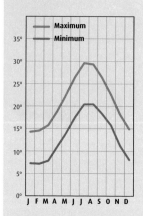

Rainfall

The local climate favours tourism nearly all the year round

White sandy beaches are typical of the southern coastline

The wild olive tree resists the wind and represents the Menorcan environment

The vegetation becomes very dense in the ravines

FLORA AND FAUNA

In the past, the most representative vegetation on the island was oak groves, but their partial disappearance has led to the domination of pine woods and wild olive trees, the ancestor of the olive tree in genetic terms, and which has been traditionally used for wood. Due to the need to take full advantage of the water available, species with impermeable leaves and evergreens dominate over annuals. Those that we might call "domestic" species and are common throughout the Balearics are on the decline: the carob tree, the almond, the fig and the olive. There are savines close to the beaches and in the damp areas.

At a second level of vegetation we can find mastichs, buckthorn, tree strawberry, heather, myrtle, heather, broom, juniper, oleander, blackberry bushes… and even closer to the ground, liliaceous plants (such as wild asparagus), arum plants (such as the unique *bec de frare*, "friar's cowl") and some curious orchids, such as the so-called yellow and blue *mosques*, "fly" orchids. We can also see beach lilies in dune areas, white and black stipa in deforested areas, or giant reeds in the wetter parts. The lichens cover the rocky spots and on the windswept coastal areas communities of dense and rounded spiny thicket, called *socarrells* (*Launaea cervicornis*). The animal kingdom is made up of, on land, small mammals, reptiles, insects and many birds. Among the former feature martins, ferrets, weasels, rabbits, bats, some varieties of field mice and the shy hedgehog. Among the reptiles are the Mediterranean tortoise, wall lizards and some small and non-poisonous snakes.

The population with most specific weight, however, is the winged kingdom: all the biotopes that can be referred to on the island have their bird population. Moreover, as summer approaches, swallows, swifts, great black-headed gulls and bee-eaters, among others arrive from the Sahara. Among the areas of great ornithological importance is Albufera des Grau, where as well as a large sedentary population, thousands of other birds come each year to breed. Keen birdwatchers can catch sight in the water, either on the shore or between the reeds, of mallard ducks, American coots, king quails, reed-warblers, storks, grebes, egrets, sharp-tailed sandpipers, pochards and stone curlews.

Common butterfly

Hairy Arum, a singular species of Araceae

Sawfly orchids

Red Horned poppy

Dominating different spaces throughout the year are also predatory and carrion birds. The intervention of man at spots where they nested has seriously reduced the number of some of these large wingspan birds. This is the case of the osprey, the booted eagle, and even the red kite. Nevertheless, falcons, kestrels, buzzards, hawk owls, Egyptian vultures and marsh harriers are all easily identifiable, as are tawny owls and barn owls.

The Egyptian vulture, *miloca* in Menorca, a carrion bird of startling plumage

The Mediterranean turtle is common in *garrigues*, thickets, and ravines

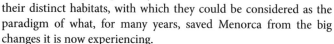

SARGANTANES

The lizards, *sargantanes* in Catalan, play the leading role in legends and songs here. There are a great many of them and there are as many varieties as there are islets scattered along the coastline (over 30). One of them, in the bay of Fornells, even carries their name. The changes, especially in colouring, have taken place precisely because of the isolation of their distinct habitats, with which they could be considered as the paradigm of what, for many years, saved Menorca from the big changes it is now experiencing.

A very unusual lizard is the one that inhabits the **Illa de l'Aire**, opposite the Punta Prima beach, in the Sant Lluís district. It is completely black and is a protected species, which years ago gave rise to the occasional kidnapping, making it the exotic star of Nordic terrariums. If you get the chance to visit the islet, you will discover that you do not have to look for them. In fact, they will approach you in large groups in search of any crumbs that may fall from a simple sandwich. It should be remembered that this a very deteriorated environment that could affect more than one species (it is one of the settings in which the s.o.m., the Ornithological Society of Menorca, www.menorcasom.net, carries out ringing on migratory birds) and you should show the utmost respect for it.

The seabed around Illa del Aire is rich in underwater wildlife

Common octopus *Octopus vulgaris*

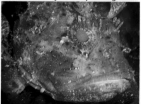

Scorpion fish *Scorpaena Scrofa*

THE MENORCAN HORSE

Horses are given special treatment compared to other livestock raised on the farms. They are the kings of the farm due to their magnificent appearance, nobility and leading role they play in the festivals. This indigenous breed of horse is startling not only for its corpulence and characteristic jet black coat, but also because of its, shall we say, "control of the situation" when confronted with the tumult and rejoicing of the *jaleo*. Young people hit them, demanding from their jockeys that their mounts do the habitual pesade on their rear legs, and these superb animals stay calm throughout. Harnessed with their finest dress, they seem to be aware of the fact that all eyes are drawn to them and they also know that their mission in this world is to create an image of singular expressiveness.

In spring, at the Es Mercadal Trade Fair Centre, the most beautiful examples are concentrated to take part in the Minorcan horse breed morphological competition.

Horses are the irreplaceable stars of the local festivals

THE "RED" COWS

The cows form an indissoluble part of the rural landscape, as do the walls separating the grazing lands. It is odd however that one can hardly see examples of the breed considered to be indigenous to the island, handsome beasts with a reddish coat. Luckily, their milk-yielding capacity has meant that recent attempts to recover the breed have prospered and now quite a few breeders have chosen to concentrate on raising this breed exclusively.

The "red" cows are of pure Menorcan stock

The springtime rainfall fills the landscape with a carpet of wild flowers

PARK OF S'ALBUFERA DES GRAU AND FAVÀRITX

NATURAL PARK
Reception Center
Rodríguez Femenías
Road Maó-Es Grau
km 3,5
turn-off Llimpa
Tel. 971 35 63 02
www.balearsnatura.com

S'Albufera des Grau is a humid area of great biological wealth, inhabited by different species of water birds as well as being an obligatory stopover for other varieties of migratory birds. Some arrive in summer to nest and feed their chicks. In its current state, it is part of the park that also covers **Illa d'en Colom** and the area of **Cap de Favàritx-Prat de Morella**. This area is considered as the central area of the **Biosphere Reserve**, which appears to have guaranteed its continuity along the lines of a conservationist sanctuary, a situation that pressure from property development had previously threatened.

The magnificent view to be had in Es Grau looking towards the sea —the wide beach, with the nucleus of cottages to one side and Illa d'en Colom to the other— continues inland and is an aspect ignored by many. In fact it is one of the most interesting spaces on the island, due to the variations from other areas at a simply contemplative

A narrow strip of land behind the beach separates S'Albufera from the sea

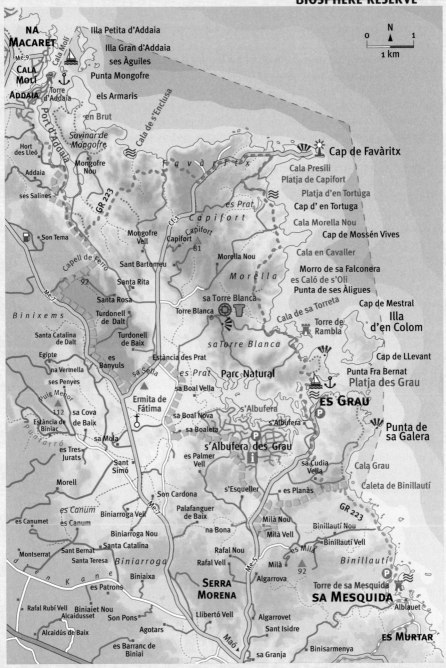

N

0 ▲ 1

1 km

NA
MACARET
Me-9

**CALA
MOLÍ**

ADDAIA
Torre
d'Addaia

Port d'Addaia

Illa Petita d'Addaia
Illa Gran d'Addaia
ses Àguiles
Punta Mongofre
els Armaris
en Brut

Savinar de
Mongofre

Cala Molí

Cala de s'Enclusa

Hort
des Lleó
Addaia
ses Salines

Mongofre
Nou

GR 223

Son Tema

Capell de Ferro

92

Me-7

Binixems

Santa Catalina
de Dalt
Egipte
na Vermella
ses Penyes

Puig Menor

112
Estància de
Biniac

sa Cova
de Baix

sa Mola

es Tres
Jurats

Morell

es Canum
es Canumet
es Canum

Montserrat

d'en Kane

Sant Bartomeu
Santa Rita

Santa Rosa

Turdonell
de Dalt
Turdonell
de Baix

es
Banyuls

sa Sella

Mongofre
Vell
Capifort

Capifort
81

CF-1

F a v à r i t x

C a p i f o r t
es Prat

Morella Nou

M o r e l l a

sa Torre Blanca
Torre Blanca

sa Torre Blanca

Estància des Prat
es Prat

Ermita de
Fátima

Parc Natural

sa Boal Vella

s'Albufera

sa Boal Nova

sa Boaleta

s'Albufera des Grau

es Palmer
Vell

Son Cardona

sa Cudia
Vella

es Planàs

sa Sella

Sant
Simó

Biniarroga Vell

Palafanguer
de Baix

na Bona

Milà Nou

Milà Vell

Santa Catalina

Biniarroga Nou

Biniarroga

Santa Teresa

Biniaixa

es Patrons

Rafal Vell

Rafal Nou

es Mila

Milà

Algarrova

92

Maó

Sant Bernat

Rafal Rubí Vell
Biniaiet Nou
Alcaidusset

Son Pons

Agotars

Alcaidús de Baix

es Barranc de
Biniai

Me-7

Me-5

**SERRA
MORENA**

Llibertó Vell

Algarrovet
Sant Isidre

sa Granja

Cap de Favàritx

Cala Presili
Platja de Capifort
Platja d'en Tortuga
Cap d' en Tortuga

Cala Morella Nou
Cap de Mossén Vives

Cala en Cavaller

Morro de sa Falconera
es Caló de s'Oli
Punta de ses Àligues

Cap de Mestral

Cala de sa Torreta

Torre de
Rambla

**Illa
d'en Colom**

Cap de LLevant

Punta Fra Bernat
Platja des Grau

ES GRAU
P

**Punta de
sa Galera**

Cala Grau

Caleta de Binillautí

GR 223

Binillautí Nou

Binillautí Vell

Binillautí

P

Torre de sa Mesquida

SA MESQUIDA

Alblauet

Binisarmenya

ES MURTAR

level; it is an incredibly valuable natural habitat for a characteristic birdlife and many indigenous plants; and because now, its classification as a **Natural Park** gives rise to scientific and educational programmes. This environment provides a wide range of biotopes: wetlands, agricultural and grazing lands, low mountain, coastal communities, cliffs, beaches and dunes. The routes suggested by the **N.P.** and the information given on the panels make it easy to situate ourselves in these landscapes, making our trips even more enjoyable with an open-air nature lesson.

The geographical centre of this area is the lake, **S'Albufera**, the water of which flows from the occasional torrents of Sa Boval and Es Puntarró, and which may be joined to the sea by the small Sa Gola canal, which acts as an overflow point which finally opens to allow the entry of sea water. Among the fish swimming in these waters are the eel, which has been fished since time immemorial, the grey mullet and the sea bass. There are crustaceans, amphibians and reptiles (singular and not at all dangerous, such as the Italian lizard), but the most apparent animal presence is made up of representatives of the winged variety. Ducks and waterfowl are in abundance, but many other species seek out their home on the small islands or fly over this "pond" of nearly 70 hectares in search of the food that makes up their daily diet. Herons, cormorants and even fish eagles can often be sighted.

Diversity is also the key word as regards the area's plantlife. The most abundant plant is the wild olive surrounding the lake. There are pine trees between the beach and the fresh water and in a section of the nearby **Cala de sa Torrreta**, as well as some tamarinds in El Prat. Hygrophila and halophyte plants, as befits a briny wetland, surround the lakeside. **Illa d'en Colom** could be introduced as a catalogue in its own right for species growing on the north-eastern coast.

In the outlying parts of S'Albufera, within the Park boundaries but on privately owned land, traditional farming methods are maintained, showing once again that balance is possible and that it embellishes the landscape.

This protected area is a refuge for many sedentary and migratory birds

S'Albufera flows into the southern end of the Es Grau beach

CAMÍ DE CAVALLS GR-223

With the aim of combining tourism and conservation, the recovery of the old Camí de Cavalls has been a great achievement and a wonderful gift for the local people and visitors alike. In its origin, linking a succession of coastal paths to achieve a circular route around the island, connecting the surveillance towers, it had a defensive purpose. But when the military use declined, this route eventually disappeared in some sections and it was the informative labour of a hardworking "Coordinating Committee for the defence of the Camí de Cavalls" that laid the foundation for it to be for public use.

The route (185 km) has been signposted throughout. The twenty stages, ten along the north and ten along the south, with different degrees of difficulty and length, makes it advisable to find out all the details before setting off on a walk (if you aim to complete the tour, you should be thinking about several days, although it is covered on bicycle and horseback too).

A walk along any of its sections is well worth it, however: its route, parallel to the sea, enables us to discover coastal sectors which cannot be reached by asphalted roads, to enter in contact with a Menorca "before" the tourist urbanisations and to conveniently breathe new life into our mind and spirit.

The Camí de Cavalls
Sergi Lara
Triangle Postals

When covering it on foot, the full tour of the island can take up more than fifteen days

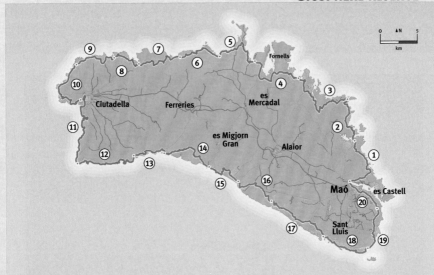

1 **Maó-Es Grau** | 10 km | Difficulty Medium
2 **Es Grau-Favàritx** | 8,5 km | Medium
3 **Favàritx-Arenal d'en Castell** | 13,6 km | Medium
4 **Arenal d'en Castell-Cala Tirant** | 10,8 km | Easy
5 **Cala Tirant-Binimel·là** | 9,6 km | Medium
6 **Binimel·là-Els Alocs** | 8,9 km | Difficult
7 **Els Alocs-Algaiarens** | 9,7 km | Medium
8 **Algaiarens-Cala Morell** | 5,4 km | Medium
9 **Cala Morell-Punta Nati** | 7 km | Easy
10 **Punta Nati-Ciutadella** | 10,5 km | Easy

11 **Ciutadella-Cap d'Artrutx** | 13,2 km | Easy
12 **Cap d'Artrutx-Cala en Turqueta** | 13,4 km | Medium
13 **Cala en Turqueta-Cala Galdana** | 6,4 km | Easy
14 **Cala Galdana-Sant Tomàs** | 10,5 km | Medium
15 **Sant Tomàs-Son Bou** | 6,4 km | Easy
16 **Son Bou-Cala en Porter** | 8 km | Medium
17 **Cala en Porter-Binisafúller** | 12,4 km | Easy
18 **Binisafúller-Punta Prima** | 7,4 km | Easy
19 **Punta Prima-Cala de Sant Esteve** | 7,3 km | Easy
20 **Cala de Sant Esteve-Maó** | 6 km | Easy

The closeness of the path to the sea provides fantastic views

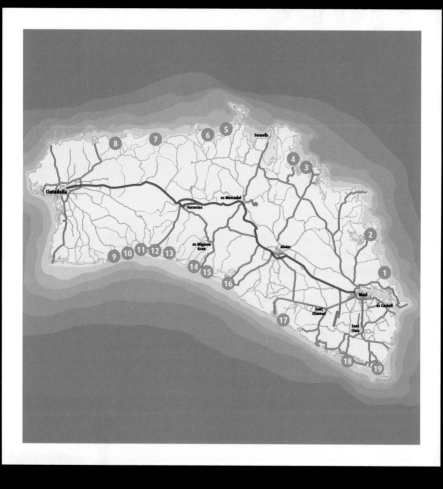

COVES AND BEACHES

Cala Macarelleta

48

Beach of Mesquida and the rocky outcrop of Es Pa Gros in the background

The defence tower and beach are farther on from the nucleus of cottages

SA MESQUIDA

This is the first substantial beach to be found when leaving Maó in a northerly direction. On arriving, the road passes between cottages that the local people began building as summer homes and which has become a picturesque centre. The beach is sandy and is framed by a rocky outcrop that rises to 68m above sea level, the **Pa Gros**, and an imposing defence tower built by the British at the end of the 18th century, due, no doubt, to the previous landing of French troops in 1781, the prologue to their occupation of the island.

Behind this outcrop appears a second cove, less frequented because there is not much beach, called **Sa Raconada Vella**.

Illa d'en Colom, the largest of the islets surrounding Menorca

Es Grau, with the beginning of the marshland and Illa d'en Colom

ES GRAU

A fabulous beach, very shallow for the first metres on entering the sea, protected by the cottages of what was a small fishing village that has evolved with time into a lively second-home holiday resort. A boat ride from here will take you to the nearby **Illa d'en Colom**, which has two charming little beaches and is the refuge for an indigenous subspecies of lizard.

There are other beaches in the same area of Es Grau, interesting due to their isolation but very small, called **Es Tamarells** and **Sa Torreta**, accessible by continuing northwards along the coastal pathway.

The most extensive beach on the north coast has many tourist facilities

Arenal d'en Castell is a very popular holiday spot

ARENAL D'EN CASTELL

Two rocky promontories frame the great sandy arch of this beach. The biggest, the **Punta Grossa**, extends out to the sea providing protection from the easterly winds for an even bigger bay where **Macar de sa Llosa** can also be found (this smaller beach can be reached walking from the Son Parc area, further to the west).

With bars and restaurants and a great deal of sports facilities on offer to fully enjoy the water sports, **Arenal** is a beach shared between the very young and family tourism. The hotels and surrounding buildings show that its adaptation to tourist needs is not a recent addition.

Son Saura in the north (Son Parc), also known as Arenal de s'Olla

The dunes of Son Saura provide some shelter to the extensive beach

ARENAL DE SON SAURA (SON PARC)

This beach has become better known for the name of the main development in the area (**Son Parc**) than for its traditional name. In part, this double name means that it is not confused with the other **Arenals de Son Saura** on the south coast (Arenal means sandy area). Before arriving by road, in a privileged wooded setting, you pass alongside the installations of the only golf course on the whole of Menorca.

A spacious beach, with all kinds of facilities, behind it lies one of the most interesting dune formations on the north coast. A lovely walk can be had by following the coastline until the tiny **Cala Pudent**, hidden in the eastern slope of La Mola de Fornells, to the left of the beach when facing the sea.

The double arch of these beaches is of a great natural beauty

The reddish tones are typical of this area of the north coast

PLATJA DE CAVALLERIA

The sandy areas of **Cavalleria** and **Farragut** are usually thought of as one single beach, taking the name of the former. They are very busy spots, despite their relative isolation, and the nearest seabed is of great interest to divers. The coppery tones that dominate the landscape here break with the insistence of greys and black, so common on the north coast.

Its closeness is the best excuse for combining a day on the beach with a visit to **Cap de Cavalleria** and the **Port de Sanitja,** one of the enclaves colonised by the Romans. The peninsula ends in a rocky outcrop and its lighthouse crowns the most northerly part of the island. From here you can see an islet, Illa dels Porros, which disappears beneath the swell when the sea is rough.

Pregondó, with Cala Pregonda in the background

The reefs of Pregonda seem to protect its heavenly image

CALA PREGONDA

To reach **Pregonda**, it is best to start in the neighbouring **Binimel·là** and walk north east along the path running a few metres from the coastline. One can feel the surprise coming up even before going over the last hillock, after which appears a magnificent setting of transparent seas, fine sands and a pine forest in the background. Its beauty has the mark of the small coves in the south, highlighted even further amidst this particularly rough coastline, and the reefs protecting it from the open sea contribute to creating a setting befitting other latitudes.

The sandy part is divided into two small beaches, the first one, when arriving by the route described takes the name of **Pregondó**.

The enormous "pebbles" of Macar d'Alfurinet

Despite its isolation, Cala Pilar is a beach with its own followers

CALA PILAR

It can be reached along the Sant Felip road, a turning off the Maó-Ciutadella road, past the km 34 mark, but you must leave vehicles parked at a point that is half an hour's walk from the cove. This route goes through a dense oak grove and is interesting at any time of the year for the views it provides; it is a northern coastal area that is still reasonably unspoilt. It is also possible to get here from **Els Alocs**, as has been mentioned.

The difficulties in reaching this spot do not stop the common presence of bathers who prefer its isolation to the crowds that gather at other points. It also has the advantage of a freshwater spring, guarded by a small figure of Our Lady of the Pilar. After the outcrop that closes off the sandy area towards the west is one of the strangest landscapes on the island. Crossing this small barrier on a short walk will enable us to take in the enormous *macs*, "pebbles", of **Macar d'Alfurinet**, a beach that seems to have been made-to-measure for the giants who, according to the legends, once inhabited Menorca.

The Es Tancat and Es Bot beaches, in Cala d'Algaiarens

La Vall has one of the best views in Cala de Algaiarens

LA VALL D'ALGAIARENS

La Vall deservedly forms part of one of the Natural Areas of Special Interest. The alluvium lands are sheltered amidst the lightly mountainous land, covered by a leafy pine forest and oak groves, and in the outlet of the old torrent appears the magnificent **Cala d' Algaiarens**. The two beaches that make up this spot go by the names of **Es Tancats** and **Es Bot**, with dune formations and an outline of marshy land behind. There is, in fact, another beach, **Ses Fontanelles**, rather hidden and more towards the open sea. Clean sands and clear waters are a lure that is difficult to avoid.

The beaches of Es Banyul and Bellavista in Son Saura. Behind, Es Talaier.

A view of Son Saura from Bellavista beach

SON SAURA

Son Saura is the largest of these coves, with a shoreline that divides it into two almost symmetrical sandy areas, the **Banyul** and **Bellavista** beaches, and with a pine forest that enables their users to escape from the heat of the sun. You reach here along the same road that leads to the archaeological site of **Son Catlar**. When the metalled road ends, in the Torre Saura Vell estate, you must continue along a stretch of dirt track before being able to park.

ES TALAIER

It is the nearest cove to Son Saura —appearing after Punta des Governador— from where it can be reached walking, passing through a pine forest. It is reached by car from a turning off the same road that leads to Cala Turqueta.

Although it is much smaller, it is a very pleasant corner, with very white sand, due to the decomposition of the limestone common to the entire area. Its name comes from the nearby presence of a very old watchtower, **Sa Talaia d'Artrutx**, from where the warning was sounded whenever intruders arrived on this part of the southern coast.

The beautiful Es Talaier beach beneath the sun's first rays

The small beaches on the south coast of Ciutadella are very busy in summer

Cala en Turqueta, between the sea and the dense wood of pines and oaks

CALA EN TURQUETA

An easterly bound boat setting off from **Es Talaier** will come across this other jewel. The only thing separating them is the rocky outcrop crowned by the previously mentioned watchtower, seen from both beaches. Whoever kept watch in it must have enjoyed enviable times... despite the isolation and the fear of pirates. Today, however, an open view of the landscape free from the human factor is only possible on a few days out of season, but it is still well worth the visit. The wood goes right down to the sea, the sand is soft and white and the waters are transparent and turquoise. The characteristics of these southern coves, so harmoniously blended, deserve our overwhelming admiration.

68

Macarelleta is a small cove, but more beautiful than many others

Macarella and Macarelleta, the latter in the foreground

MACARELLA AND MACARELLETA

The musical air of their names accompanies the heavenly image that these coves leave imprinted in our minds. Macarella rests in the gap of the cliff that the water from the ravine has slowly enlarged on its way to the sea. **Macarelleta** is hidden in another fold, to the right of the former, both near and far if you go on foot, because the path between them is not very direct.

On the **Macarella** beach are caves used in prehistoric times as burial chambers... and in more recent times as summer homes for the first one to get there. There is a restaurant and the cleanliness of the beach is controlled. From Ciutadella it can be reached by car going towards **Sant Joan de Missa**, turning off there to reach the Torralbet estate, where the last stretch is taken before reaching the car park. From Cala Galdana it can be reached on foot by going through the wood.

Galdana has been a symbolic area since the tourist boom took off

The spectacular Cala Galdana, with the last part of the Algendar ravine

CALA GALDANA

It has the fame of being the most spectacular on the island, even with the tourism. This cove boasts a singular beauty with many shadows, projected from the buildings —that have not managed to completely shroud it— and its occupants themselves: the hundreds of summer bathers mean that you can hardly see the sand on the beach except for the odd patch between towels, sun loungers and paddle boats. We should, however, forget the comments of those who knew it before it was unspoilt —there's no looking back— and enjoy as much as possible the magnificent arch of sand and the whole setting.

This is the point where the **Barranc d'Algendar** ravine ends, a natural area of great worth. A shelter for animals and indigenous plantlife and, at one time, fertile orchard lands. With the changing uses that modern times have brought about, its estuary has become the landing jetty for the area. At the opposite end of the cove is a raised hill, **Penyal Vermell**, which gives us a view from Sa Punta, with excellent views of the beach, inland and the open sea.

Overall view of the Mitjana and Mitjaneta coves

Cala Mitjana is the first of several unspoilt coves east of Cala Galdana

CALES MITJANA AND MITJANETA

The smallest is a mere bend with sand at the foot of the path from which it is reached walking from Galdana. These two beaches are, however, well worth visiting for their isolation and beauty. Some people consider them to be nudist beaches but those wishing to wear a swimming costume may do so.

Between these two beaches and the Binigaus beach, though there other scenic beaches but more difficult to get to, you have to walk or go by sea. They are the beaches of **Trebalúger**, **Fustam** and **Escorxada**, all three within the Es Migjorn district.

Binigaus, a nudist redoubt, at the end of a section of cliff-lined coast

Binigaus beach, at the estuary of the ravine of the same name

BINIGAUS

From **Sant Adeodat**, walking west, the waters and sands of **Binigaus** are reached, particularly appreciated by nudists and sun-worshipers wishing to tan themselves far from the madding crowd. A narrow corridor of dunes separates the beach from the cultivated fields, and only by passing the widest point, at the outlet of the Binigaus ravine, do the cliffs begin gaining height again. This is the most crowded sector because there is a sun lounger service and beach bar and at the rear, the pine forest reappears, providing an escape into the shade when the sun becomes just too much. A short walk through this pine forest will take you to **Cala Escorxada**.

The islet of Binicodrell marks the boundary of Sant Adeodat beach

Sant Tomàs beach

SANT TOMÀS AND SANT ADEODAT

These beaches are the outlet to the sea of **Es Migjorn Gran** and its greatest tourist attraction. Located on a strip of very low southern coastline, it extends from the islet or stony ground of Binicodrell to the Punta d'Atàlitx, corresponding to the sector closest to this point, to the east, called **Sant Tomàs**. The urbanisation also goes by this name, with several hotels and an expanding development. In contrast, the section opposite the point where the road changes direction and becomes the main street corresponds to **Sant Adeodat** beach. Parallel to this and forming the beach's border is a very pleasant pedestrian walkway.

Both beaches, confused as being one because the symbolic separation of the projection called Punta Negra is quite reduced, share services and are highly recommendable for families to enjoy to the full.

Son Bou is, logically, one of the busiest tourist enclaves

Son Bou beach: kilometres of sand looking southwards

SON BOU

The longest, 4 km, and most visited beach. The sandy part goes from Punta d'Atàlitx to Cap de ses Penyes, bored through by caves that have been fitted out. At the foot of this headland, to the left of the beach if we are facing the sea, the remains of a Paleochristian basilica can be visited (see p. 148). Due to its width, **Son Bou** is by and large the domain of groups of bathers, with children, parasol and inflatable Lilo. The beach is also served with spa services, hire of sun loungers and nautical objects and many other facilities at the back (among them a water games park).

Despite the heavy development, it has managed to save the adjoining wetland, **Es Prat**, which was once used for growing rice.

Aerial view of Cales Coves, an excellent refuge for sailors

The caves in the cliffs have given it its name of Cales Coves

CALES COVES

The two small coves are reached by taking a dirt track that leaves from the **Son Vitamina** urbanisation. This spot, where three ravines flow into the sea, is famous for the strange make-up of the landscape and the existence of niches of a prehistoric necropolis, dug into the walls of the cliff. In one of these caves Roman religious inscriptions were also found dating from the 2nd century AD. Visited by backpackers and small leisure boats, it is one of the spots that most comes to mind when talking about the "wild" side of the island. Until very recently, the projects to adapt the setting to tourism clashed with an unexpected occupation of the caves: in hippy times a heterogeneous community had discovered how comfortable they were to live in.

A bend of sand in the middle of a rocky area

Binibèquer beach

BINIBÈQUER

With fine sand and clear water, protected by a stony piece of ground that projects into the sea, it is the most frequented beach in the Sant Lluís district. This is partly due to the supply of services, including the age-old beach café with bar and restaurant.

Also nearby, but to the west of Binibèquer, is **Cala Torret**, an urbanisation without a beach but with harbour installations and terraces from where it is possible to jump into the water.

Punta Prima provides its users with a vast sandy area

PUNTA PRIMA

Years ago, **Punta Prima** was one of the favourite spots for the local population to spend their holidays. The small huts remain from those days, some of them with a small garden. Later with the rise in tourism, the hotels appeared, new streets were opened and the number of chalets increased. In its most recent phase of growth a macro-complex has appeared which has resulted in the seasonal population being doubled.

The beach and the waters that lap it seem to be the same, but seeing the setting of this delightful *Sandy Bay* (the name given to it by the English) full to overflowing with people, many Menorcans ask themselves whether, in the third millennium, any aspect of the Menorcan landscape hardly disturbed by man will remain.

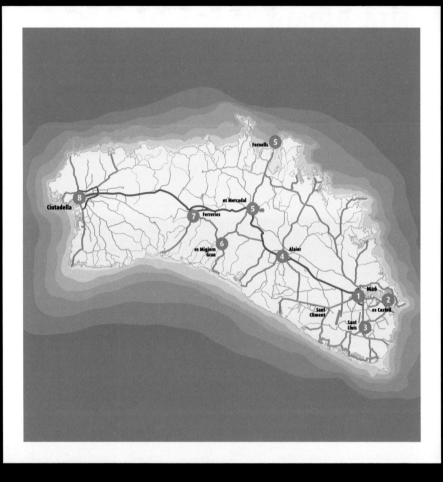

THE ISLAND, TOWN BY TOWN

Alaior

MAÓ

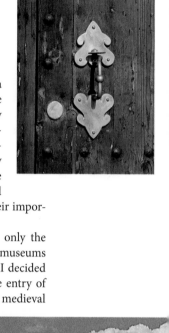

Over the last twenty-five years, Maó has experienced a
series of urban improvements which have renovated the
city. Of all these improvements, the restoration of many
public and private buildings deserves a very special mention. Maó is reconciled with its past and offers it to its visitors with justifiable pride. With the new millennium hardly
under way, the buildings that marked its growth from the
18th century onwards shine out again like beacons, adapted
with total naturalness to the new times and recovering their importance in the modernised centre.

Of the Maó prior to the Catalan-Aragonese conquest, only the
occasional references we can come across in books and museums
have survived. Between that year of 1287, when Alfons III decided
on the consolidation of the existing fortification, and the entry of
Barbarossa in 1535, there had been an expansion in the medieval

Panoramic view of the city from the far side of the harbour

The inhabitants of Maó built their summer houses on the opposite shore

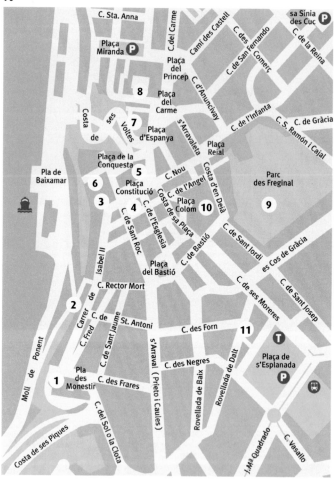

**POINTS OF INTEREST
IN THE OLD QUARTER
OF MAÓ**

1
Museum of Menorca
2
Cas General
(Military Government)
3
Ajuntament (Town Hall)
4
Principal de Guàrdia
5
Church of Santa Maria
6
Public Library
7
Mercat del peix
(Fish Market)
8
Municipal Market
9
Parc des Freginal
10
Teatre Principal
11
Scientific, Literary
and Artistic Society

centre that forced the defences to a second wall; after 1600 this boundary would also be moved. It was, however, British domination, by making it the capital, which produced many of the changes that can still be identified today, two centuries later. On any city tour we embark on, we inevitably come across the stamp of that period.

A fine place to start would be the **Pla del Monestir** in order to visit the church and cloister of Sant Francesc, which today houses the **Museum of Menorca** (see p. 108-111). Firstly it was a convent, and the church was built throughout the 18th century, which would explain its Baroque decoration over an out-of-phase Gothic approach, useful, nevertheless, for building in stages. Once the architecture and contents have been seen, it is a good idea to do a tour of the remodelled exterior in order to take in a view of the port, the driving force behind the previously mentioned transformations, and the **Dalt Vilanova** district to the west.

From there, the route continues along the Carrer Isabel II, with the stately homes and hanging galleries (the lansdcape that dominates the Levante wharf), and the **Cas General**, the residence chosen by Kane and which today is the military headquarters. It ends at the convent of the Conception-ists, leading to the neo-classical facade of the **Town Hall**. To see it from the front you have to go into the **Pla de sa Parròquia**, Plaça de la Constitució. This area, invaded every day by vehicles who have to park somewhere, awaits the annual festivities whose noise is as deafening as that of the traffic, but far more vibrant.

Also in the square stands a military building, the **Principal de Guàrdia**, and the **church of Santa Maria**, the construction of which began in 1848 where there had previously been a church of the same name that Alfons III had ordered to be erected. On the outside, only the bell tower, built a century later, alleviates a little the heaviness of

Tourism has meant a change of use for the buildings of Baixamar

the disproportionate monument. The inside, however, is embellished by the angelic appearance of the enormous organ. Built by the German masters Otter and Kirburz and fitted with 3,210 pipes and four keyboards, it bedazzles anyone who comes to listen to the concerts given by famous international artists; it is even considered to be one of the reasons why the people of Maó have such a passionate love of music.

The Pla de sa Parròquia leads to the **Plaça de la Conquesta** through the narrow alley dedicated to Alfons III, of whom there is also an effigy in the square. So much repetition is inevitable in the very heart of the castle, the fortress where the Muslims surrendered and which produced medieval Maó. The palace of **Can Mercadal**, turned into the Public Library, and the viewpoint beyond this building, make the visit to this part well worthwhile.

On leaving the square by the opposite corner to the entrance we come across the **Ses Voltes** coastline, the main entrance point to the city from the sea. From here a descending walk spreads out towards the wharves, a park-cum-archipelago of leafy islets that seem to have emerged from among the meanders of the grey asphalt river. For those having to ascend the successive sections of steps, the viewpoint changes. The gradient and the walls of the cliff-side are quite impressive, along with the very concept of the original project (1951, Josep Claret), but the latest interventions in this space —also known as **Parc Rochina**— have softened the intimidating effect.

Carrer de Alaior, at the end of the old walled Maó

The buildings overlooking this garden, the **Casa Mir**, inspired by Modernism, and the **Peixateria**, the working fish market are all the work of the architect Francesc Femenías. The author of many original houses, warehouses and factories, he was also responsible for important civil works in his role as municipal architect.

Leaving a visit to the port as a specific tour in itself, the next stage has to be, due to its closeness, the series of buildings known as **El Carme**. The convent that housed the Carmelite order, later a courthouse and prison, has been transformed into a series of spaces for cultural purposes, among which features the building housing the archives of the **Fundació Hernández Mora**. The cloister remains the home of the meat, fruit and vegetable market, which had previously occupied this space for more than a century, and below the central courtyard a new commercial area has been created, connected to the underground car park of the plaça Miranda. This square has another splendid view across the port, and from the adjacent Plaça

del Príncep and Carrer Anunciavay one can reach the pedestrian centre that includes the streets of **S'Arravaleta** and **Nou**, the steep slopes of **Deià** and **Hannover** and the **Plaça Colom**, with the small streets that extend from it. This area, full of shops, gives you an idea of how the tourist season is doing by simply observing the flow of people in and around it.

Just on entering the Deià slope you come across the gateway-passage to the **Parc des Freginal**, a garden area of modern design and heir to the bygone divisions of communal orchards.

The Deià slope culminates at the **Teatre Principal**, opened originally in 1829 to house opera performances (it is even older than the Liceu in Barcelona), and another mainstay of the local love for theatre and music. A short distance away, in the Plaça Bastió, the towers of the **Arc de Sant Roc** are the last standing witnesses to the second ring of defensive walls.

We must make a detour on the route, however, by placing ourselves in another street of longstanding tradition, that of Doctor Orfila or **Carrer de ses Moreres**, from which start Carrer Cifuentes

The organ
in the church of
Santa María, pride
of the city

Costa de sa Plaça (or Hannover) is one of the busiest streets in the town

Pla del Carme

and Carrer del Cós de Gràcia. In the latter, an old path to the **hermitage of the Verge de Gràcia**, patron saint of the city, is where the spectacular equestrian competitions of the annual festivals are held. One of the notable buildings of the Cós is the **church of the Concepció**, built as an orthodox temple by the Greek colony that arrived in the city... also in the 18th century. If one takes into account the fact that there was also a Jewish synagogue and that the other large temples are from the same period, one can deduce that there was great prosperity and that the abolition of the Inquisition by Kane gave rise to religious freedom enjoyed by many denominations.

The Carrer Cifuentes (or Sa Rovellada de Dalt) has been mentioned before: here is the **Scientific, Literary and Artistic Ateneo**, or Society. This society, which continues to promote numerous cultural events, houses an important collection of algae and fossils.

S'Esplanada could end this basic circuit of the historical part of the city... and similarly may be the starting point, since it is kilometre zero as regards communication between Maó and the rest of the island. There is a new bus station where there was once the British barracks and over what was once the parade square pigeons now flutter. Young people make dates, the elderly stroll and the clothes

The old Teatre Principal has also been recently renovated

and handicrafts market attracts crowds twice a week. Despite the fact that here the uses and spaces have been reorganised with specific projects, the vitality generated continues to nourish daily life. It is the perfect spot for giving your feet a rest and taking in the route covered so far.

We must, however, move on, because that described so far does not mark the end of the long list of interesting things to see. Streets such as S'Arraval, Camí des Castell, Gràcia or San Fernando are centres of other possible routes in order to discover, adjacent to the industrial estate, a modern, entertaining and didactic area, the **Parc Rubió i Tudurí**, which throws light on local plant life. Therefore, depending on the time you have available, don't hesitate to "lose yourself" by turning in any direction: it will be well worth it.

PORT DE MAÓ

The exceptional length of Port de Maó is shown in this picture

This name not only designates the stretch of sea that penetrates the island for over five kilometres: it is widely used to encompass the entire area it covers, although, administratively speaking, part of it belongs to the district of Es Castell. It is this geographical accident that has sufficient entity in itself and autonomy for it to deserve special attention. It marks the geological division of Menorca into two highly differentiated parts, as has been mentioned, and has been the driving force of progress in key moments in the island's history. Sandwiched between two shorelines of a very different aspect and height, this domesticated sea was already a coveted shelter in ancient times. It was baptised, according to legend, by the Carthago Magón Barca, Hannibal's brother. Andrea Doria, one of Charles V's admirals, paid the famous homage to its favourable conditions, saying that, "it was the best port in the Mediterranean… along with the months of June, July and August". The British opened it up to intercontinental trade —securing for more than a few residents of Maó the fortunes that would enable them to build houses that are still today termed as "palaces"— and it housed the very first US base in Europe.

Maó, due to its dominating position, has some unbeatable views from different points of the city, especially along the **Passeig Marítim**, the seafront that goes from the Plaça Miranda to the avenue of Fort

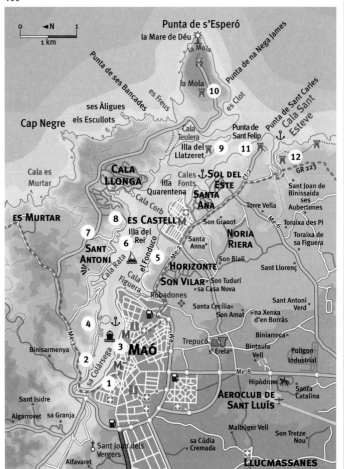

Punta de s'Esperó

POINTS OF INTEREST
AROUND THE PORT
DE MAÓ

1
Sa Colàrsega
2
Cós Nou
3
Maritime Station
4
Naval Base
5
El Fonduco
6
Illa del Rei
7
"The Golden Farm"
8
The Cemetery
of the English
9
Llatzeret
10
La Mola Fortress
11
Sant Felip Castle
12
Fort Marlborough

de l'Eau (echoes of the migration to Algeria and other places are perceptible even in the street names). From this avenue you can now go down to the one that continues by the port in a public lift just a few metres from the Club Marítim. Or go up the other way, of course. The boat-trips are also recommendable, providing a complementary and very direct view. There is so much to see, however, it is almost inevitable that we must move around on land. From **Sa Colàrsega**, the most distant point from the mouth of the inlet, you can start two different routes —possible on bicycle— so as to see the most interesting of its two banks. On the north shore, **S'Altra Banda** for the Maó locals, the road that goes to La Mola passes behind the Cós Nou, a goods harbour, the power station and the **Naval Station**, and over the summer chalets of **Riu Pla** and **Cala Rata**. At the top of Cala Sant Antoni, overlooking all of this shoreline, the red house of the Sant Antoni estate appears in sight, more commonly known as **The Golden Farm**, a beautiful building and with the fame —improbable though widely rumoured— of having housed the love trysts of **Lord Nelson** and Lady Hamilton. If we drop down to sea level, on

A team of volunteers have worked to recover the buildings on the Illa del Rei

either side of the **Casa Venècia** can be seen two small and pictur-esque cemeteries. One is called the cemetery "of the French" and the other "of the English", although in this latter one, the majority of graves are those of American marines. Opposite is the **Illa del Rei** (Bloody Island for the British, because of the military hospital they built there). Continuing towards the enormous fortress that Isabel II ordered to be built on **La Mola** (see p. 107), Cala Llonga is crossed and the Llatzeret on its isle can be made out, once a penin-sula (see p. 129).

The other walk, on the south shore, passes first by the **Ponent** (Western) harbour —where the **Maritime Station** is located— and the **Llevant** (Eastern) harbour, widened at their confluence in the **Pla de Baixamar**. In this little square, at the foot of the old quarter, some sculptures by Gaspar Servera contemplate their fate. Along the winding route you will see that the trade of yesteryear has once again returned. In the basements now occupied by shops, restau-rants and trendy bars, it is not uncommon to find ceilings sup-ported by enormous beams rescued from the shipyard breakers' yards. They once housed warehouses or workshops of the *mestres d'aixa* (artisan boat-builders), who built solid craft. The setting has changed as much as has nautical engineering with increasingly more sophisticated sailing boats and yachts that moor on the jetty where the *Mô* mermaid (a piece of work by Leonardo Lucarini) lives, and which houses the **Club Marítim**.

After passing the terraces it seems that the port ends, but after a bend **Cala Figuera** appears and further on **El Fonduco**, a very peaceful spot. In the former of these two areas was La Industrial Mahonesa, the pioneering factory of the textile sector.

Returning, and going up to the road that leads to Es Castell, we can finish this route around the south shore with a visit to the above men-tioned spot and the nearby points of interest. Just on leaving Maó we pass in front of the Hotel del Almirante, which gets its name from hav-ing once been the residence of Admiral Collingwood when he had his leave on land. In Es Castell the perimeter facing the sea is a very inter-esting stroll, and when we leave, it is worth visiting **Fort Marlborough** in Cala Sant Esteve and the remains of Sant Felip Castle, planned by Calvi, the great 16th century military fortress engineer.

In recent years, the presence of tourist cruisers passing through or mooring in this stopover is constant. Large ships bearing all the flags of the world add their passengers to the great flow of tourists that

The fading sunlight caresses the 18th century buildings of the naval base

The old hospital of the British navy on Illa del Rei

already move around the city from the early hours of the morning. Their visit often includes a stroll around the most attractive parts of the island, which explains the fleets of coaches that take them around parked by the harbour. The majority of cruise passengers, however, spend their brief stay on a walk around the city, giving top priority to a shopping expedition.

EXCURSIONS AND VISITS IN THE PORT DE MAÓ

The **Yellow Catamarans** of the Berguiners company cover routes around the Port of Maó for one hour. During the tourist season twilight and night trips are programmed with live singing and a glass of cava.
Tel. 971 35 23 07 / 639 67 63 51 | www.yellowcatamarans.com

The large **Don Joan** ship of the De la Cruz company, makes trips for a stroll and a swim in either Illa d'en Colom or Binisafúller, north or south, according to the weather.
Tel. 971 35 07 78 / 626 00 41 54 | www.rutasmaritimasdelacruz.com

From the 1 of May to the 31 of October, trips around the port of Maó are also organised on the **Water Taxi** boat, which has its mooring in the Cales Fonts jetty, in Es Castell. Up to 10 passengers (minimum 2) can board and it offers other services, such as transfers to La Mola, El Llatzeret or the Illa del Rei.
Tel. 616 42 88 91 | www.watertaximenorca.com

This building housed the former customs office
Sports boats occupy the moorings of Moll de Llevant

THE FORTRESS ISABEL
II, LA MOLA
MAÓ
Tel. 971 41 10 66
www.fortalesalamola.
com

THE FORTRESS ISABEL II, LA MOLA

The **Isabel II Fortress**, on the peninsula of La Mola, is the military construction of greatest historical and architectural value on the island of Menorca. Strategically situated in the mouth of the port of Maó, it was built in the second half of the 19th century to replace the castle of San Felipe, a fortification situated on the opposite shore and which was destroyed in 1782 after long resistance by the British garrison who then defended it.

La Mola, as the whole complex is popularly known, had lost interest for the local population since it was no longer used for military purposes. However, its restoration has meant that, after years of abandon, its vast installations now receive a large number of visitors, and is now a not-to-be-missed point of interest in the tourist sightseeing circuit. Endless galleries, moats, underground water deposits, ramps, terraces... the stonework and the rocky beauty of the enclave still gives one a thrill and enables us to delve into a not too distant past. It is a highly recommended visit.

In its interior, there are many details that add architectural interest to this fortification.

MUSEUM OF MENORCA

Touring the rooms of this museum is a delight not only due to the beauty of many of the pieces on show and the atmosphere of the setting itself, but also because its contents provide the information for clearly understanding the island's reality through its historical evolution.

MUSEUM OF MENORCA
Maó
Doctor Guàrdia, s/n
Tel. 971 35 09 55

The old Franciscan convent that houses the museum has been the object of a long and laborious process of restoration and adaptation in which, at the same time, the relationship between the building and the city has been improved. The outside has been worked on at regular intervals to provide a resting and walking area along with the panoramic viewpoint over the port —adjacent to the church of Sant Francesc— which was already there.

The Museum's archives are now displayed in a manner befitting their value. Over the more than one hundred years since the opening of the Municipal Museum of Maó, its predecessor, it has had different homes and many ups and downs. The items have finally been given the importance they deserve, putting them within reach of the local and visiting public in order to comply with their educational and informative function. There is an uninterrupted supply of new pieces found in archaeological digs or from loans or donations from various sources.

The first lesson is a result of the chronological order these archives are placed in. The first floor is given over to the most distant cultural references which includes the Pre-Talayotic and following period, until arriving at Roman and Byzantine times. There are spaces devoted to the two extremes of this wide spectrum in time as well as the intermediate periods: Talayotic culture and contact with other Mediterranean cultures (prior to the Roman conquest). One can thus appreciate the evolution from very primitive forms to the notable refinement of the Roman and Byzantine cultures, from stone through to metals, the path between the utensils

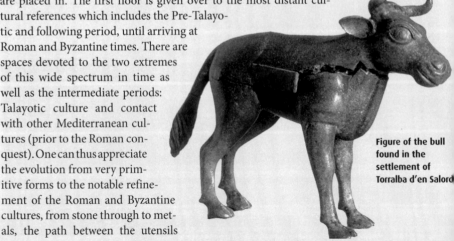

Figure of the bull found in the settlement of Torralba d'en Salord

A spectacular painting shows the wharves of Maó in the 19th century

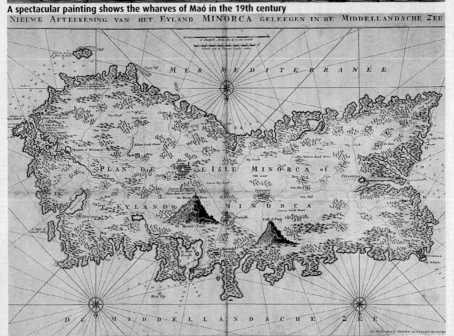

NIEUWE AFTEEKENING VAN HET EYLAND MINORCA GELEEGEN IN DE MIDDELLANDSCHE ZEE

A curious representation of the island, opposite to the normal interpretation found at Cales Coves and the bust of Tiberius (a replica, since the original is in the National Library of Paris).

These rooms house colossal mortars, Roman anchors, amphorae for marinades and carts for transporting salted meat and fish. Outstanding, however, are two small bronze figures: one representing Imhotep, a secondary Egyptian deity who was an architect in his human form and a doctor as a God, assimilated to Esculapio; and the other, in the form of a calf and just as ready—one supposes— to be worshiped, since bullfighting was already widely extensive in the ancient Mediterranean. The life-size bronze horns, also on show, seem equally suitable for bullfighting celebrations.

Muslim and medieval Menorca is represented in the first room on the second floor. There is less material on display (due to the destruction of patrimony suffered during attacks from the Turks), but there are some very spectacular items such as the two-faced cross from the chapel of the Santa Àgueda Castle. In the adjoining gallery are images of saints and a Station of the Cross, all with ceramic support, used as decoration for the building when it was the Convent of Jesus, before confiscation in 1835.

The room given over to the 18th century reflects the prosperity and opening-out to the outside world during the years of British and French occupation, with the help of day-to-day objects —crockery from different sources, apparel and tools— and the invaluable pictorial documentation by the masters Chiesa and Calbó. The interest that the items provide is by no means diminished even though they are closer in time to the present. On the contrary, they are in fact more curious. A display cabinet, for example, shows the important growth of the Masons, who had seventeen lodges on the island. In another, a collection of caricature figures gives us an idea of life at the end of the 19th century. The map collection, with maps of all the nationalities that played some role or another in the formation of Europe between the 17th and 20th centuries, shows the strategic importance that Menorca was given.

The tour ends with an anthology of 20th century painting by both Menorcan and foreign artists who have had an intimate relationship with the island. There are works by Hernández Monjo, Vives Llull, Torrent, Sans Huguet, Arnulf Björndal, Josep Vives, Quetglas, Fedelich and Pacífic Camps, among others, providing a magnificent final touch to everything on show here.

Small statue of Imhotep, from Torre d'en Gaumés

Inner courtyard of the square cloister

Stone plaque honouring the arrival of Alfons III, "the good King of Aragon"

AROUND MAÓ

In the eastern part, **Maó** is the main reference point for any type of activity. As well as the specific routes around the city and the Port area (see pages 99-105), also recommendable are all the routes that, by wandering beyond the city boundaries, enable us to discover the outlying area. Here though, for reasons of space, we can only refer to the trips that go north, with the same starting point as that described on page 133 (dealing with eastward trips of the south shore).

The first of these tours (starting off, we repeat, from Maó) could be the journey to **La Mola**. The visit to the fortress of Isabel II, La Mola, is reason enough, but there are also different spots along the way to enjoy great views of both Maó and Es Castell, and the walled perimeter of Llatzeret overlooking the isthmus of Els Freus. When returning, just at the point when taking the right detour towards **Sa Mesquida** —completing this trip—, the whole area can be appreciated even better. It is a hilly area carpeted with low and sturdy vegetation where, according to some people, the very best camomile in Menorca can be picked. In order to start a second stage towards the **Es Grau Natural Park** you must return to the port of Maó.

The road towards **Es Grau** turns off from the Fornells road shortly after passing the orchards of Pla dels Vergers or Sant Joan, which are on the left. The road ends amid a nucleus of cottages, alongside the beach, and then extends to **S'Albufera**, a humid area of great biological and landscape interest (see p. 40-43). The park can be visited from here on foot, and the Illa d'en Colom, beyond the bay, by boat. But its furthest point, **Cap de Favàritx**, so it is better to reach it by car. To do this, you should go back along the way until reaching the junction with the Me-7 and follow this road until reaching the Hermitage of Fàtima, at kilometre 8. Some five hundred metres from the sign you must turn right onto the Cf-1. The direction to follow is marked by a strange rocky outcrop, standing alone on the flat, which is called **Sa Sella** (saddle). At the end of this road is Cap de Favàritx and the lighthouse of the same name, with its peculiar landscape of black slate sculpted by the erosive action of the sea. The beaches of **Presili** and **Tortuga**, located to the south of this point, can be reached by an unmetalled track.

MAIN COVES AND BEACHES

Sa Mesquida
See pages 48-49

Es Grau
See pages 50-51

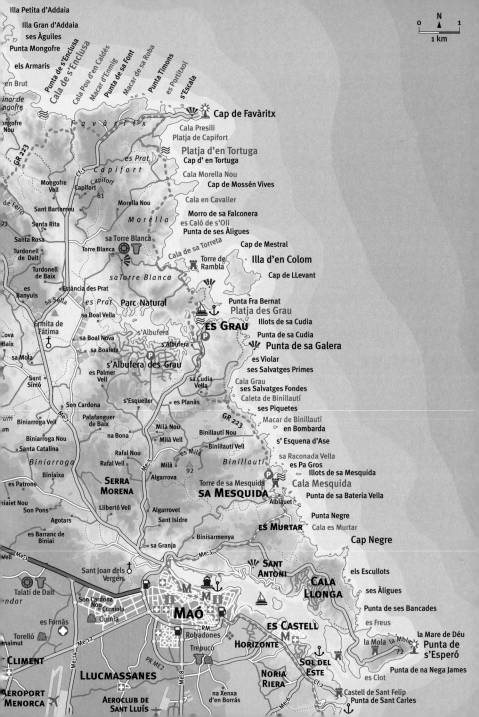

Don't forget that on the routes that involve taking the main road, you can also visit several archaeological digs such as **Talatí de Dalt**, **Rafal Rubí** or **Biniac**.

RAFAL RUBÍ

The prehistoric funerary buildings known as *navetes* get their name from their similarity to the shape of an upside-down hull of a boat. The oldest, dating back to the pre-Talayotic period, are oval or circular, but later evolved into more elongated forms, as is clearly shown in the most famous one, the ***Naveta* des Tudons** (see p. 195). Of no less beauty or constructive quality are those that may be visited near to the main road shortly after leaving Maó. The biggest one preserves the lintel through which the two inner levels can be reached.

Close to Rafal Rubí you can also see those of **Biniac-La Argentina**, western and eastern, the latter being very small and without its roof, but nevertheless really interesting.

TALATÍ DE DALT

This is one of the spots where regular digging work and studies are undertaken, young people arriving every summer from all over to continue working on the site of the settlement. The variety of elements, with the existence of hypostyle halls, artificial caves, half-buried dwellings, as well as remains of a megalithic enclosure, lead us to believe that it was an important settlement in its time. There are two talayots, one made of flat trapezoidal stones, and the enormous *taula* providing a lateral appendix that could be interpreted as a supporting pillar.

Entrance to one of the *navetes* of Rafal Rubí

Settlement of Talatí de Dalt

SA TORRETA

Located within the **S'Albufera Natural Park**, its *taula* is the only one remaining on the northern side of the island. Not only is it quite spectacular in itself, with an enormous vertical stone over which rests a smaller horizontal one, common in all of these constructions, but the landscape it overlooks is also incredible. From where it stands it has an unbeatable view inland and along the coast, with **Illa d'en Colom** standing out on the horizon. Very nearby, going down towards the sea, there are other remains, among which feature a square-shaped *naveta* called **des Figueralet**.

You can reach the dig from the cove of Sa Torreta (walking from Es Grau it takes half an hour and enables you to see the Rambla defensive tower over the rocky outcrop that closes the small cove **es Tamarells**). Another way is through the Torre Blanca estate, along a path to the left that leaves the road and leads to Favàritx (a detour of the Maó-Fornells route as well).

TREPUCÓ

This settlement, which can be reached from the city centre of Maó, must have been one of the biggest on the island in its time, extending nearly 5,000 m². One of its talayots, the most visible, is also the biggest among those still standing. There is an area with a *taula*, circular and rectangular dwellings, fragments of walls that were raised as a defensive measure, and part of two square towers on the west wall. The remains can also be recognised of another pentagonal wall with bastions that were built by French troops in the 18th century in order to prepare for the attack on the mythical fort of San Felipe.

Taula of Sa Torreta de Tramuntana
Taula and talayot of Trepucó

BINIPARRATXET PETIT

The fact that archaeological remains can be admired as soon as one arrives at Menorca airport, next to the car park to be exact, is symptomatic of the wealth of the area in materials of this kind. It is a section of the **Biniparratxet Petit** dig, excavated and moved to its current position in 1995 in order to avoid its disappearance due to the extension work on the runway. Thanks to its meticulous reconstruction, one can see a very complete Talayotic dwelling, joined by an uncovered central courtyard and part of the hypostyle hall attached to it, used as a storeroom-larder. In the dwelling, the spaces are clearly defined according to their use, documented by the numerous organic remains and ceramic pieces that were found. What stands out, however, is the hearth and the cistern for collecting rainwater.

TORELLÓ AND ES FORNÀS

These two spots, which are very nearby, are reached by taking a path that leaves the road going to Sant Climent on the right, after passing the roundabout for the airport. In **Torelló** there is a magnificent talayot, being one that contains a raised inner chamber, with clear later additions that converted it into a watchtower.

In **Es Fornàs** we can see the remains of an interesting early Christian basilica of Byzantine influence, with a single prolonged nave in a square apse. It possessed a hemispherical baptismal font and stunning floor tile mosaics. The space that would have been known as the *sanctuarium* features figures of a peacock, a symbol of resurrection, and a lion.

Archaeological dig of Biniparratxet, alongside the airport

Talayot of Torelló

Es Grau

Sant Climent

The swell emphasises the rugged coastline of Far de Favàritx

The Cap de Favàritx protects the beach of Presili from the northern winds

Cala en Tortuga, a marvellous reward after the effort of arriving on foot

PRESILI AND TORTUGA

Cap de Favàritx marks a point of inflection between the north-eastern coast and that which receives the direct battering of the Tramuntana wind. The lighthouse, erected over black slate rocks, overlooks a fantastic landscape created by the thousand shapes it sketches, but it may become Dantesque and aggressive when hit by northern storms. Before that, however, there are two beaches that face east, **Presili** and **Tortuga**, included in the same area protected by the S'Albufera Natural Park and highly appreciated by those looking for corners "uncontaminated" by tourist installations. Behind the second beach there are dunes and some marshland.

Further on from Tortuga, towards the south and passing the outcrop that separates them, you can reach the beautiful and little known cove of **Morella Nou**.

Cala Morella Nou is reached on foot from Tortuga

ES CASTELL

During the second occupation of the island by the British, it was decided to transfer the inhabitants of S'Arraval Nova (the nucleus surrounding the Sant Felip Castle) to a new part. The streets of **Es Castell** —originally named **Georgetown**— grew around the parade ground that we know today as the **S'Esplanada**. In this town centre the barracks reveal the town's military origins even after their use has been changed (the engineers' barracks now houses the Military Museum). The monotony of great white blocks of military architecture is only broken by the Town Hall building, painted red and with a tower that protrudes from its main facade. The interior small

Projecting from the wharves of Cales Fonts, Es Castell looks out to the sea

square is of interest here, with rooms around it that were used as a meat market and children's school until it was recovered for local government purposes.

The same location of the parish **church of Roser**, just outside the town centre, shows the priorities of whoever designed the village. Construction work began on the church in 1777 in neo-classical style, but its inside houses a stone altarpiece that dates back to a much earlier period.

Recent civil works in **Es Castell** have focused on recovering seafront spaces that had gradually lost importance in other periods, such as Moll d'en Pons, Cala Corb or the Moll de l'Hospital. This emphasises the sea's role in the original urban planning, where the main streets led to the coastline and the individual houses —many of which are

Torre Stuart, known popularly as the Torre d'en Penjat (hung)

Aerial view of Cala Sant Esteve; Fort Marlborough can be seen on the right

still standing— had large gardens with views across the inland sea of Port de Maó. Until now, and undoubtedly in the future, **Cales Fonts** can boast of the only real seafront. The old fishermen's harbour was one of the first parts of the island reconverted for tourism: bars and restaurants occupy the caves that were storerooms and refuges and their terraces stand where once the fishing nets were mended. The noise and hurly-burly during the summer months does not affect the popularity of this spot even after other poles of attraction appear on the scene. There is no competition from the diminutive **Cala Pedrera**, with hardly any sand, hidden between the urbanisations of Santa Ana and Sol del Este, or from **Cala Corb**, which thrusts deeply into the selfsame town centre. Nevertheless, the improvement of all these spaces will undoubtedly renew the town's image.

AROUND ES CASTELL

CALA SANT ESTEVE

As in other small coves close to town centres, the residents who own a cottage in the area are the main users of **Cala Sant Esteve**. More than its leisure facilities, what makes this cove special is the strategic role it has played at specific moments throughout the island's history. Its name comes from the fact that it was here where the relics of St. Stephen were landed in the times of Bishop Severo, resulting in a great many conversions from within the Jewish community.

On its south side is **Fort Marlborough** and further on, the **Stuart tower** or **d'en Penjat**, fortifications erected by the British in the 18th century. On the other side, on the Punta de Sant Carles and opposite La Mola, stood the legendary Sant Felip Castle, demolished on the recovery of Spanish sovereignty. In this latter setting in summer there are night-time guided visits with a period atmosphere (see page 238).

FORT MARLBOROUGH

The first thing the British did after occupying the island was to strengthen their defences, even before signing the Treaty of Utrecht, since their dominion, together with that of Gibraltar, ensured them full control of the Mediterranean. This small fort, very modern for its time, had to protect the southern flank of Sant Felip Castle, which in turn acted as a defence for Port de Maó. Its name was given in homage to an illustrious soldier of the time, General **Sir John Churchill**, Duke of Marlborough. Its central square is a large pit excavated out of the stone and, on being below ground level, is very well hidden in the surrounding countryside. It is entered by a tunnel that opens out to the southern shore of Cala Sant Esteve and a tour of the fort uncovers a great many details of civil and military life at the time it was in use. With the aid of modern technologies, there is an exhibition outlining the circumstances of the sieges to which the French and Spanish troops subjected it and the alliances and confrontations between the powers that marked the life of Menorca in the 18th century.

FORT MARLBOROUGH
Es Castell
Cala Sant Esteve
Tel. 971 36 04 62

Fort Marlborough defended the island from the southeast

ILLA DEL LLATZERET

This fortified area was built as a quarantine for people with contagious diseases of a certain level. It is therefore made up of different areas and several buildings, one of which still houses old medical instruments and other curiosities. The construction was completed in 1800, but the land it is built on was a peninsula of the northern shore until 1900, when it became an island due to the works for St. George's Canal, or the Alfons XII Canal. Until recently it had been used as a summer residence for civil servants who work for the Health Department and their families. It also plays host each year to the Public Health Summer School, where leading experts in health matters attend from all over the world. It could be said, then, that its current use, also health-related, is not too far away from its original function.

Materials from the ruined Sant Felip Castle were used to build it

SANT LLUÍS

The creation of this town of rectilinear streets was the responsibility of the Count of Lannion, the French governor who had a good public image amongst the Menorcan people. The eighteen blocks that were then planned, in the mid-18th century, have been overtaken by very recent additions, with the same impetus that has made tourism the town's main activity. It is the town that has grown the most in recent years, along with Ciutadella.

A watercolour painting by Giuseppe Chiesa —a great visual chronicler of his time— shows that the church and obelisk in **Pla de sa Creu** had already been built before there were houses around them. The project of the French, as well as providing homes for their troops, aimed to provide an organisational centre for an extensive rural area that was relatively highly populated. A central location was chosen in the free space that existed between the already standing farmhouses. The church, which still today attracts the attention of the viewer in the middle of the network of two-storey houses, is in a neo-classical style, with an explicit dedication on the front that asserts its intention to honour St. Louis, the French king.

Another building from that time is the flourmill whose silhouette forms one of the most typical images of the town. Two towers from old mills are still preserved, as well as a *pou de torn*, a well, which served the people living in Carrer del Comte de Lannion. An interesting walk is around the farmhouses surrounding the town (**Es Pou Nou**, **Torret**, **S'Ullastrar**…), where the characteristic traits of rural architecture can still be appreciated. This is due, to a great extent, to the fact that many of the houses have been converted for residential use and the new owners have had them restored with few changes.

As well as the coves that will be mentioned later on in more detail, there are other points on the district's coastline where you can swim or sunbathe, such as the Biniparratx or Binidalí coves, which also provide excellent shelter for boats. There are rocky areas where not a grain of sand exists —such as **Cap d'en Font**— but they are still very popular due to the limpid transparency of the water that laps them.

The church was one of the town's first buildings

An ancient Menorca lives on in the farmhouses, at least in the forms

In the Sant Lluís district many rural images can still be seen

The walks in the Levante area —the north east section— which have been shown on pages 112-114 have their logical counterpart in a route along the southern coastline, taking in the whole **Sant Lluís** and **Es Castell** coast. If starting off from Maó, you should firstly head towards Sant Climent (on the same road with the turn-off to the airport that ends in Cala'n Porter). Once in Sant Climent, the first stage of a south-eastern tour will involve spending time in **Cala Canutells** and its environs, in order to get your bearings to continue on to **Binidalí**. Here there is a marvellous viewpoint from the clifftop. The cove, along with that of **Biniparratx** that lies immediately after, is the most sheltered of this stretch. Afterwards, as from Cap d'en Font, the high profile of the coastline softens and drops. Going along the roads that connect the urbanisations, which gradually link up with each other, you reach the **Binissafúller**, **Binibèquer** (the biggest of the three) and **Biniancolla** coves, all with beach bars or bars and restaurants nearby. Before reaching the second cove we come across the unique urbanisation of **Binibeca Vell**.

The last beach on the section is **Punta Prima**, which has the **Illa de l'Aire** opposite, with its lighthouse and population of black lizards. In the Sant Lluís district, however, we can still visit **Cala Alcalfar** and **S'Algar** by turning off the road that goes from Punta Prima to the town.

Before returning to Maó, the last stopovers should be **Cala Sant Esteve**, where you can visit **Fort Marlborough**, and Es Castell (see p. 124-128), taking advantage to enjoy the atmosphere of **Cales Fonts** if arriving at twilight. To get from Sant Lluís to Es Castell through different scenery, you should take the road that passes by the Trebalúger farmhouse.

ETHNOLOGICAL MUSEUM

There are three old mills still standing in Sant Lluís from the time when boats from other parts still approached the island to transform their cereals into flour. Located at the entrance to the town if coming from Maó, the biggest and most spectacular houses a small museum containing an attractive collection of old tools and utensils. These objects illustrate close-up what life was like in bygone times and shows trades that have slowly disappeared or evolved with time. The mill, completely restored in 1987, rounds off the lesson since it also shows off the perfect working order of its machinery which is occasionally set in motion. On the ground floor, as well as the ethnological museum rooms, there is a tourist information point.

ETHNOLOGICAL
MUSEUM
Sant Lluís
Es Cós, 4.
Tel. 971 15 10 84

The mill is still in condition for grinding grain

AROUND SANT LLUÍS

BINISSAFÚLLER

The palm trees that close off the ravine and the old huts alongside the small jetty bring to mind the character of a private oasis that this cove must have had before the urbanisations besieged it. On either side of the enclave, spots such as the tiny **Caló Blanc** or **Caló Fondo** are also great for refreshing yourself by way of a large natural pool.

BINIBECA VELL

The tourist complex of Binibeca Vell surrounds the nearby **Caló d'en Fust**. Given the name of "fishermen's village", it is much visited for its unique architecture, reproducing the irregular forms and anarchic layout of many old small villages on the shores of the Mediterranean.

MAIN COVES AND BEACHES

Binibèquer
See pages 82-83

Punta Prima
See pages 84-85

Binissafúller beach

Biniveca Vell

Caló d'en Fust and the tourist complex of Binibeca Vell

ALCALFAR

The first hotel on the island specifically focused on tourism was built in this small cove, although some residents of Sant Lluís already spent their holidays here. You can notice this family atmosphere and the limited space from the style of the huts that are grouped around the cliff and between the cliff and the road. Only one shore is urbanised and on the other a watchtower stands out, adding a lively note to the picturesque setting. Between the **tower of Alcalfar** and the one overlooking the neighbouring Punta Prima, called **Son Ganxo**, you can walk by following the ancient **Camí de Cavalls** footpath, easily passable here. If you try the route the other way, you must set off from the old saltworks alongside the beach, separated now from the tower by the urbanisation (see longer excursion on pages 214-215).

S'ALGAR

Located over a point along the coast that drops down to the sea, this old urbanisation is often cited as an example of sensible and restrained tourist development. It is made up of privately owned houses, rented apartments and two hotels, the lack of a beach being compensated for by all kinds of leisure and sports facilities. The sand there is of a purely testimonial nature, but the platforms built over the stony ground make swimming possible.

Furthermore, anyone daring to go beyond the limits of "civilisation" has the chance to discover a small jewel of "unspoilt" nature behind them: the last section of the **Barranc de Rafalet** ravine, occupied by the oak grove and with an incredibly beautiful view of the cliffs that protect the outlet.

Cottages in Cala Alcalfar with "garage" for the boats on the ground floor
Urbanisation of S'Algar; behind it is hidden the tiny Cala Rafalet

ALAIOR

This city —as it deserves to be named since being awarded the title by Alfonso XII— was created at the expressed desire of another king, Jaume II of Majorca, in 1304, when the parish of Santa Eulària already existed and in order to group together the inhabitants scattered in the outlying area. A farmstead called **Ihalor** is documented as previously existing in the area, a name that is often used instead of its current one.

Throughout history it has always maintained its independence, almost always irrespective of the orders that Ciutadella or Maó tried to impose on it, settling for the tertiary position behind them in the never-ending battle for the role of leading city. It gained this independence, which it still defends, with its *universitat* institution founded in 1439, the title which for over three hundred years guaranteed its self-governing status at a municipal level.

The church of Santa Eulària, in Alaior, overlooks an ocean of rooftops

It could be said that tourism entered the island via Alaior: the **Cala'n Porter** urbanisation was the first and that of **Son Bou** did not take long in filling the pages of the first travel brochures in which Menorca appeared. This priority activity is not very noticeable in the town centre, however, perhaps because some kilometres of almost unspoilt scenery separate it from its satellite urbanisations. In mentioning it, the outskirts of the town are great for bicycle trips, especially towards the north, where one of the spots worth visiting is the hermitage of **Sant Llorenç de Binixems**, a traditional destination of local processions.

The recent widening of the main road has hidden the image it once offered a little, but whoever enters Alaior from Maó can still take in the "everlasting" view of a hillside of houses crowned by their main temple of worship. The **church of Santa Eulària** dominates and imposes, built in the highest part of the town in order to gain respect and obedience, symbolic or otherwise, for the role it plays or played in the people's lives. The first work dates from the 14th century, but there was a rebuilding process in the 17th century that corresponded

to the Baroque details. A little gloomy inside, the outside dazzles in contrast, exposed to the sun that illuminates it, and the winds, but as solid and well ensconced as can be seen from some aspects of the building: the curious turrets on the main facade or the buttresses, reinforcing its castle-like aspect.

Sant Dídac, a Franciscan church and convent, is another notewor-thy building. Its ancient cloister, known as the **Pati de la Lluna,** or Moon courtyard, is especially beautiful, even with its separation into housing units (and steps are being taken to turn it into a public space of varied uses). The **Can Salort** building, full of character, currently houses a part of the UIB, the University of the Balearic Islands.

A detailed walk will enable you to discover not only the most obvi-ous and immediate —the streets making up what has always been "the centre", those closest to the Plaça Nova, the Carrer Major or the Town hall, with an imposing entrance— but also the views to be had from its historic boundaries. Close to the church is the **Munt de l'Àngel**, with its water tower competing with two old mills and square forming both a car park and viewpoint. It looks out to the south and the east and, further on, to the ravine broken up by orchards. This southerly view uncovers a blue horizon. Indeed, from Alaior you can see the sea.

The Pati de sa Lluna, before the houses become to public spaces

Still in the urban north-east, another square shaded by pine trees, that of the hermitage of **Sant Pere**, marks the cemetery exit, with the **Es Cós** as the obligatory direction. On this walkway over another gradient, today facing the industrial estate, the galloping horse races of the festivals take place, and it is the last path in the town for the people of Alaior. The ledges on the stone walls that line it provide the public with a raised grandstand from which to view the equestrian competition.

Although the district is chiefly known for its connection with the tourist industry, and secondly for its footwear manufacturing —with world famous brands— its original link with the countryside and country chores has not been lost. The annual agricultural and livestock fair, with breed competitions and exhibitions of machinery, reflects the vitality of the dairy industry, directly linked to these sec-tors. The cheese manufacturers have modernised production meth-ods and greatly enlarged their markets, and as all the brands provide

MAIN COVES AND BEACHES

Arenal d'en Castell
See pages 52-53

Arenal Son Saura
See pages 54-55

Son Bou
See pages 78-79

Cales Coves
See pages 80-81

produce of an unquestionable quality, buying this typically Menorcan product for your own consumption or as a souvenir or gift is highly recommended.

AROUND ALAIOR

Leaving Alaior towards the south, a local road goes to **Cala en Porter** and passes by the prehistoric settlement of **Torralba d'en Salord**, where you simply must take a look at the magnificent *taula* and series of remains that surround it. It also brings us close to **Cales Coves**. When reaching the crossroads with the Sant Climent and Maó road, you simply have to decide whether you turn right or left, depending whether you start from one or other of the coves mentioned. Both should be visited, so close to each other but so far apart in many ways, marking the end of some ravines that appear to be deeper than they actually are due to the imposing nature of the high walls that encircle their course.

Going southwards again, the recommended stop on the way to **Son Bou** is the **Torre d'en Gaumés** (see next page), and Son Bou deserves a stroll to see the remains of the Paleochristian basilica. This can be done before or after taking in the whole view from the highest part of the urbanisation.

Towards the north, entering into a pretty wooded area, is another road, the Camí Vell d'Alaior. It goes towards **Port d'Addaia**, with its long and narrow bay of over 3 km; the holiday village of **Na Macaret**, long appreciated by the people of Alaior who have a cottage and boat there; and the beach and urbanisation of **Arenal d'en Castell**. To get from here to **Son Parc**, which, as before, is an important tourist complex, you must return until reaching the Maó-Fornells road, from which there is a handy turning (recognisable by the leisure installations installed on a former piece of farmland). Once again, the scenery brightens up our route. Son Parc plays host to the only operating golf course in Menorca, as well as several apartment complexes that surround the magnificent beach of Son Saura del Nord or **Arenal de s'Olla**.

Another interesting route is to go to, or return from, Fornells when in Alaior and is one that goes to the **Sa Roca** urbanisation. This route provides a contrast of the seascape with the inland scenery, discovering woods of holm oak and pines, on land that gains height until reaching Puig de s'Ermita at 218 m.

One should take into account, of course, the many possibilities provided by the **Kane Way** (see p. 151). We would add that any trip to Maó or Es Mercadal in which you are in no hurry is always more pleasant along this route. It also has some unusual views, such as the one over Es Mercadal when crossing the Pla d'Alaior, with strange rock formations sticking out of the flat land. It is an area of livestock farming.

TORRALBA

As in many of the prehistoric settlements, the one at **Torralba d'en Salord** was also occupied during the Roman period and in the Middle Ages, but the analyses carried out show that the most notable constructions were already there before 1300 BC. Standing out amongst the whole complex is the enormous *taula* and the sanctuary area surrounding it in the shape of a horseshoe. This area revealed the remains of votive objects —among them, a small bronze bull— which are currently owned and exhibited by the Museum of Menorca. It is precisely the presence of these items that has made academics produce the hypothesis that the *taules* were symbols of divinity and not a simple architectural solution.

You can also see (the "urbanisation" of the space makes it a highly accessible visit) a very large talayot, Pre-Talayotic houses and other areas whose probable use was for storing or as a deposit. Near to these excavations you can see those of **So na Caçana** and **Torre Llisà Vell**, although without the same facilities.

TORRE D'EN GAUMÉS

Another very important settlement very extensive in size, the talayots are visible from the road when travelling from Alaior to Son Bou. Here was found another small figure of great archaeological value representing the Egyptian demigod Imhotep. Despite the fact that no *taula* remains standing, a capital was located and the corresponding premises can be seen. There are also many houses, hypostyle halls and remains of walls. A little further south is the megalithic sepulchre of **Ses Torres Llises**.

The *taula* of Torralba is one of the biggest on the island
Area around the *taula* in the settlement of Torre d'en Gaumés

THE PALEOCHRISTIAN BASILICA OF SON BOU

Its age, dating from around 5 AD, and its location, next to the beach, make the visit to this basilica both justifiable and easy, close to the caves dug out from the Cap de ses Penyes. They once formed a necropolis in prehistoric times and the sacred nature of the spot must have lasted and influenced the choice of the site by the early Christian community.

The layout and items that have been preserved correspond to the most common model in the period of North African influence (Vandal kingdom of Carthage). The building, with a single nave and rectangular ground plan, is built in an east-west direction; the portico was in the west, with three entrances. Featuring here is the baptismal font, hollowed out of a single block of cylindrical stone in a lobular-shaped cross.

The Son Bou basilica, on the most eastern part of the beach

THE KANE WAY

The first British rule of Menorca began with the landing of General Stanhope's troops in 1708, during the Spanish War of Succession. One might have thought in those days that the British presence would have been episodic, but five years later their occupation was approved by the **Treaty of Utrecht** and the Menorcan people had to accustom themselves to the desires of their new rulers. Generally

speaking, they respected the customs and improved the living conditions of the population and one of their leading figures in particular has gone down in history as a benefactor of the island and promoter of progress and peace. This was **Richard Kane**, whose influence, firstly as deputy and later as governor, was noted until his death in 1736. Kane converted Maó into a great naval base and moved the capital from Ciutadella, but not without opposition from the clergy and the nobility. He also regularised the census and established rules for controlling weights and measures, and laid special emphasis on improving the road network and developing agriculture and livestock breeding.

Kane, immortalised by Chiesa

A monument, recently moved to the start of the road between Maó and Fornells, at the height of the Vergers de Sant Joan, pays homage to him. A little further on, on the left, a turning presents us with the **Kane Way**, one of his major contributions. This road, which in its time was the main road that connected the island, today has a secondary role but is nevertheless of great interest in terms of scenery. Using it as an alternative route in some trips enables you to discover some curious details of this countryside. It is also the base for making short excursions to the hermitage of Binixems, for example, or to the Sa Roca urbanisation (these turnings are before and after reaching the Alaior cemetery). The fact that this is not a fast road means that it is also a good route for those groups travelling by bicycle.

PORT D'ADDAIA AND NA MACARET

In this case one could complain that the text should not be placed alongside others referring to coves and beaches. The charm of the area justifies its inclusion, however, to describe an area where there is a beach, albeit a very small one, in **Na Macaret,** and a marvellous shelter for boats, **Port d'Addaia**, whose entrance, it is true, requires a certain skill to navigate around the rocks and islets that guard it. Between both points is another shelter **Cala Molí**, where some folk from Alaior have their boats moored and which was perhaps the origin of the development in a very family-like setting.

The plantlife of the marshes on the shoreline tell of the presence of fresh water. This is because, in the past, the water that arrived from the small ravine had its outlet here and worked the mill, or *molí,* that gave it its name.

Na Macaret is a small haven on this section of coast

CALA EN PORTER

The extensive sandy area of this cove, patterned with parasols and rows of hammocks during the peak season, is a golden strip separating the sea and the wetlands where the ravine ends. It was one of the very first coves to be developed for tourism. Some natural caves in the cliff were fitted out for a discotheque, **Cova d'en Xoroi**, whose name comes from a beautiful but tragic legend from the area. A spectacular spot with spectacular views, it can also be visited during the day.

Cala'n Porter was one of the very first tourist beaches

ES MERCADAL AND FORNELLS

ES MERCADAL

The bell tower of the church of Sant Martí dominates this town situated in the island's central area, at the foot of its highest point, mount **El Toro**. Its location made it an obligatory refreshment post when travelling was slow, but there are many locals and tourists who carry on the tradition (with the excuse, for example, of entering the town to buy some typical cakes in Ca's Sucrer, an establishment of merited fame).

In the past it was the main town of a very large district —including the original towns of Es Migjorn and Ferreries— and had the privilege of holding a market —from where its name derives— once a week. With the same simplicity of its oldest houses, the eminently rural nature of the area is still perceptible, where the number of people who sowed the seed in the fields was much higher than the

View of Es Mercadal from the hills surrounding the town

number who lived in the town. Urban growth in recent years has practically doubled the land space that was occupied before, but the centre itself has hardly changed. Unique constructions that stand out above the rest include the great *aljub* or tank and the flourmill transformed into a restaurant. The *aljub* is another of the contributions to the communication system and public services that were introduced during the mandate of Sir Richard Kane on the island (see page 151). It was built by Pere Carreras in 1735 and with its enormous collecting and storage capacity of rainfall, it solved the water supply problems of a good many local people.

The **Centre Artesanal** (craft centre) of Menorca and the Multifunctional Hall are the palpable demonstration of the care given to the cultural reality of the island.

Before reaching Es Mercadal coming from Alaior, you can see, alongside the road, on the height known as **Penya de s'Indi**, an unusual sight. It is a monolith in which fractures and erosion have naturally cut out the form of an Indian chief wearing a feather headdress.

The mill, alongside the main road, is now a busy restaurant

In summer, every Thursday from 7 to 10:30 p.m. the colourful handicrafts market is held in the Plaça Pare Camps: items of pottery, flowers, painted clothes, *avarques* (country sandals), wickerwork and forging on display with the festive accompaniment of dances and live music.

FORNELLS

The bay of Fornells casts a spell over whoever contemplates it for a second too long. A shelter for fishermen returning from the rough seas, its protective role has been extended to the summertime over-crowding: it fires emotional phrases to fill postcards, rocks the efforts of beginners facing the winds on surfboards or in small boats and distracts the digestion of the gourmets. It is like a huge saltwater lake purposely placed to relax the senses. It is the scenery and soul of this small town that transmits peace and calm and which, how-ever, arose from the shelter of a fortress, the Sant Antoni Castle. Like the Sant Felip Castle, at the entrance of Port de Maó, and for the same strategic reasons (contrary, of course, to those who had recom-mended its construction), it succumbed to the pickaxes. Only some of its storehouses remain, appearing alongside the shore when we enter the town, and which cannot be confused with the solidity com-municated by the restored British watchtower that guarded over the entrance to the bay.

From its privileged position, **Fornells** is ideal as an operational base for sea trips along the north coast, a coastline where delightful little corners alternate with very hard coastal furrows. It is also the desti-nation of all good food lovers, who sometimes even arrive from the other islands, drawn by the steaming aroma of delicious *calderetes de llagosta* (lobster stews, and many restaurants are commissioned to promote this dish).

The tiny hidden coves on the shore opposite the town —from where you can also try and walk along the **Mola de Fornells**, pro-tected as a natural space— or the old saltworks, at the innermost point of the bay, are others among the many attractive possibilities offered by the area. To reach these spots you need to cross the watery stretch, which can be made on boards or kayaks for hire, because the water is usually calm and navigation is easy here.

British watchtower

The still waters of the bay with El Toro in the background

The cottages facing the harbour make up an idyllic scene

AROUND ES MERCADAL AND FORNELLS

MAIN COVES AND BEACHES

Platja de Cavalleria
See pages 56-57

Cala Pregonda
See pages 58-59

The ways converging on **Es Mercadal** still allow for direct contact with the agricultural Menorca of bygone times. The best views are obviously to be had from **El Toro**; the brave and adventurous might like to climb it via a turning from the Kane Way (shortly before entering the town if coming from Alaior), thus being able to better appreciate the characteristics of the land. The old **Tramuntana path** slips away to the north following the undulation of the hills and uncovers beautiful scenery. By this route, via the entrance to Cap de Cavalleria and the beaches that will be described in the following pages, it is possible to see the *basses* (small lakes) of **Lloriac** (normally in winter and only if it has rained a lot), an enclave visited by many birds taking advantage of the water collected due to the not very porous ground. Also well worthy of a walk or bicycle trip is the section of the **Kane Way** that leaves Es Mercadal towards Ferreries, just four kilometres, and which passes through a dense oak grove. and those of the Camí de Cavalls connecting the beaches of **Farragut** and **Binimel·là** and the latter with **Cala Pregonda**.

The municipality has marked other interesting coastal walks around **Son Parc**, **Fornells**, **Arenal d'en Castell** and **Tirant**, a great excuse to stretch your legs and clear your lungs.

**Boats in Sanitja:
the twilight frames
a peaceful moment**

General view over Fornells and Ses Salines

El Toro

The barely 358 m height of **El Toro** stands out above a basically flat landscape. Although legend tells that it was a bull with silver hooves that showed the presence of a black virgin at the bottom of a cave, the patron saint of Menorca, the name comes from the one given to it by the Arabs, al *thor* (the mount), or the pre-Roman term of *tor*, which means the same.

When pirate incursions were still frequent, its fortification was started in order to provide refuge for a population that today approaches it for spiritual reasons or for the views, which on clear days, take in the Mallorcan coast.

The imposing silhouette of El Toro dominates the Menorcan countryside
Entrance courtyard to the church and convent on the top

Cala Tirant

On the other side of the peninsula to that where Fornells continues to grow, turning our back on it, this beach has always been linked to the population of the bay. The developed space has also been increasing, a reflection of the interest that the area has aroused and the good positioning of the nucleus of more crowded constructions on one of the rocky hillsides. This part is reached by a road that starts close to **Ses Salines de Fornells**, but the beach is easier to reach by an unmetalled road that leaves the road to Cavalleria.

The beach maintains the interesting aspects of yesteryear thanks to its extension and to the concentration of houses alongside the sandy area. Behind, a marshy land is still maintained where tamarinds grow.

Binimel·là

A turning from the old Tramuntana path leads to this large and comfortable beach, today a metalled road until the final part. It is, however, quite manageable. The entire route from **Es Mercadal** may be considered to be of scenic interest, as is the beach, despite some past attempts to develop which still spoil some views. Today it is protected by being included in the Natural Area of Special Interest that goes from Els Alocs to Fornells. If you have time, you can walk to the **Farragut** and **Cavalleria** beaches, or only as far as the intermediary Cala Mica. You could also walk inland to the lands of **Pla Vermell** (*vermell*, red, due to the colour of the soil), where the presence of fresh water provides a glimpse of fertility amidst the dry stony ground.

Behind the beach of Cala Tirant a small marshland survives
Binimel·là is a large and accessible beach, with a unique setting

Cap de Cavalleria and Sanitja

The **Cap de Cavalleria** occupies the northernmost end of the island. It is a spot well worth the visit, given the spectacular nature of the high cliff and the views it offers us of the coastline and the islet opposite the outcrop, **Illa des Porros**, as well as seeing the imposing lighthouse, for which reconversion plans are already under way: a room devoted to sea studies and a permanent exhibition about the marine reserve that makes up this section of the coast will be up and running shortly.

Roman coin found in Sanitja

From the *cap* we can clearly see the rough orography of the peninsula it crowns: the east and north-facing sides are high with cliffs, whereas in the west-facing part the base of the peninsula gently drops towards the port of **Sanitja** and the sea.

Here was where the Romans built a settlement (100-300 AD) that was originally of a military nature, later taking on commercial and urban characteristics. It is highly likely that there was already a stable population here in Talayotic times, but its existence since Roman times are documented by the discoveries of many objects during archaeological digs and from the writings of the naturalist

The lighthouse of Cap de Cavalleria and Illa dels Porros

and scribe Pliny the Elder, who mentions it as having the status of *civitas* and the name of Sanicera. It is also thought that the Roman generals landed here with their *foners*, experienced slingshot soldiers, hired as mercenaries for their wars. In the accounts of the many battles won by the Roman Empire, the bravery, skill and strength of the Balearic slingshot soldiers, used as shock troops, is famous.

In the land surrounding this small port, archaeological prospections are regularly held that for some time were connected to the **Ecomuseu de Cap de Cavalleria**, which, in an accessible and educational way, exhibited pieces of great ethnological value, which helped us to understand singular aspects of the setting from Antiquity until today. The heads of these excavations still hope that they will be able to show the remains discovered in a new location.

Port of Sanitja, with the defence tower in the background

Cap de Cavalleria, with the Port de Sanitja on its left slope

ES MIGJORN GRAN

The *Gran* (great) that features in its name may seem a mite excessive to the outside observer, but the use of the adjective should not be attributed to an ardent megalomaniac. The name in fact refers to its condition of "capital" of a large and fertile area: the *migjorn* (midday). It also responds to the pride of the local inhabitants who know that their ancestors built the oldest houses that we see today in a setting where human presence has made its mark since prehistoric times. It is not surprising, therefore, to feel the sensation that both the properties and the residents having been there "forever".

The small church, devoted to St. Christopher

When entering the town from Alaior or Es Mercadal, the road runs parallel to the beginning of the Binigaus ravine, enabling you to see the hillside crops on scaled terraces contained by dry stone walls. There were already houses in the Carrer Major (High Street) in the 17th century. The locals who built them belonged to the parish of

Colour brings the very old houses back to life

Ferreries, a spot which at that time had the fame of being rather insalubrious, and when the population grew they approached the idea of building a small church as a necessary step in achieving legal independence. They took a long time in achieving it, despite their conscious awareness of belonging to an independent town.

Despite the fact that **Es Migjorn** has grown in a similar way to other towns on the island, its partial isolation over many years can still be read from the old layout of short streets and the houses which are sheltered in them.

A much-loved and remembered figure in the town is **Francesc d'Albranca**, the pseudonym used by the celebrated folklore expert Francesc Camps i Mercadal to publish his anthologies of Menorcan traditions and legends. The local music band is also highly appreciated, and in recent years has enjoyed great popularity (it is the favourite band for livening up the local annual festivals of many towns). This brings us to once again underline the passion for music of the local people, among whom there are families that could even form their own orchestras with so many instrumentalists in their ranks.

AROUND ES MIGJORN GRAN

Woods and agricultural and livestock farms surround **Es Migjorn Gran**. Of the latter, the most curious is undoubtedly that devoted to ostrich raising, close to the road to the town from the turning off the main road (between Alaior and Es Mercadal). Speaking of roads, it should be stated that the sections leading directly to Ferreries and Es Mercadal, although they are not so comfortable, are both highly interesting due to the remarkable scenery they offer.

The area is very uneven and with dense vegetation, up to the point where in summer it maintains the greenness that other parts of the island begin to lack. The characteristic landscape of the ravines dominates the south, which in this area differs from the usual coastal profile, high and with cliffs, when **Binigaus** is reached.

When you go down towards the sea in the direction of the **Sant Tomàs** and **Sant Adeodat** beaches, you can take the turnings leading to the prehistoric settlements of **Santa Mónica** (to the left of the road) and **Sant Agustí** (to the right). In the latter there is an interesting Talayot hollow with a huge wooden beam, something that is not present in the others. There is also an interesting archaeological excavation in **Binicodrell de Darrera**, located at the start of the old Binigaus path which leads from the cemetery.

MAIN COVES AND BEACHES

Binigaus
See pages 74-75

Sant Tomàs and Sant Adeodat
See pages 76-77

Example of a country landscape in the *migjorn* area

FERRERIES

This town did not achieve official recognition and segregation from Es Mercadal until the mid 19th century, despite its medieval origins. Its name is connected with the blacksmiths that perhaps already existed when Jaume II of Majorca awarded the original centre the category of parish. Other nearby places also take their names from similarly-related activity, such as **S'Enclusa** (the anvil), a small hill, which with **Santa Àgueda**, another notable "peak", gives a "mountainous" aspect to the countryside.

The progressive change to new economic activities has turned its appearance upside down in barely the last twenty-five years; undoubtedly started off by the adaptation to tourism of **Cala Galdana**. Today, the local people work in construction and in the furniture, imitation jewellery and footwear factories, gradually distancing themselves from the traditional agricultural way of life. These transformations have given Ferreries a new lease of life, but the flavour of yesteryear has not been lost. It can still be sensed in the small streets surrounding the parish **church of Sant Bartomeu** and in the remodelled Plaça Espanya where, on Saturday mornings, the handicraft and agricultural market is held.

Close to the town, by a turning on the road to Es Migjorn Gran, is the prehistoric archaeological dig of **Son Mercer de Baix**, wih a series of pre-Talayotic dwellings among which feature one that goes by the name of **Cova des Moro**. It is a very primitive *naveta*, or chamber, with a roof of stone slabs resting over stone columns, smaller at the base and becoming larger as they rise towards the capital. From this point you can go down to the neighbouring ravine of **Sa Cova** and take in a marvellous sight of its confluence with the Trebalúger ravine.

Marking the boundary between this district and that of Ciutadella, another ravine, the **Barranc d'Algendar**, is undoubtedly one of the most startling natural spaces on the island. Between the Pla Verd, where it begins, and the Cala Galdana, where it ends, its high walls protect highly fertile orchards and corners where the water and exuberant vegetation create unforgettable landscapes.

The old town was tightly packed around the church

Tradition, colour and flavours in the Saturday market

AROUND FERRERIES

The Ferreries district runs between the north and south coast and therefore possesses very contrasting scenery. It is also the area with the highest average altitude, close to 140 m above sea level. In the south, the coastal outline —between **Cala Galdana** and **Cala Trebalùger**— is also higher than on the rest of the of the *migjorn*, with high cliffs only broken by the beaches already mentioned and those in the middle of **Mitjana** and **Mitjaneta**. An outstanding geographical accident on this coastal section is called **Pont de n'Ali**.

MAIN COVES AND BEACHES

Cala Pilar
See pages 60-61

Cala Galdana
See pages 70-71

Cala Mitjana and Mitjaneta
See pages 72-73

From the town to the sea, the land is packed with pine forests that lean over the deep schisms of the ravines. The fertile land, protected from the rough winds of the Tramontana, watered by the rain collected by its basins and with the fresh water from some springs, have made the ravines —going back to the period of Muslim domination— the ideal spot for growing fruit and vegetables. Their names, **Sa Cova** (or **Son Fideu**), **Son Granot**, **Santa Maria** or **d'Algendar** remind whoever discovers them of idyllic images of fresh orchards; and also of dense and wild vegetation amongst which a privileged wildlife is sheltered and fed. In Menorcan folklore there is a very nostalgic song devoted precisely to a young wife who got lost in these paradises, **Algendar**, after being abducted by a daring Moor.

And of course, on reaching the fine white sands of the beaches, you encounter the emerald reflections of incomparable waters.

In the north are dense oak groves and high views, such as those that can be had from the **Ruma path**. From Ferreries, in a northward direction, this path passes by the Hort de Sant Patrici estate. Passing a section of curves which gradually gain height, you reach the houses that make up Sant Francesc. If you leave the car here and take the unmetalled track to the right, you reach the main attraction of this route: a very open view enabling you to see the two coastlines of the island. Now approaching the north, the track becomes a footpath after passing Sant Josep. It becomes easy and flat once again on the section coinciding with the **Tramuntana path**, starting the return route until reaching Sant Antoni de Ruma. From this point onwards, as you continue climbing there are some magnificent views again of the side of S'Enclusa and **Santa Àgueda,** another interesting spot to visit outside Ferreries that is covered in detail on pages 222-223.

Els Alocs

The same road that takes you Santa Àgueda also goes to Ets Alocs, although the metalled road ends on the Binigaufà estate. It is a locally used beach but interesting for the surrounding scenery. A path halfway up the cliff —part of the Camí de Cavalls path— enables you to walk to the neighbouring **Cala Pilar**. In the opposite direction, towards the east, is **Cala en Calderer**, but it is much further away and the path disappears amidst the vegetation.

Puig de Santa Àgueda, in the background of a Ferrieres landscape

For many people Els Alocs is just a passing point to reach Cala Pilar

CIUTADELLA

The "other capital" of the island is equally attractive and hospitable, qualities that during the high season of the tourist calendar take it to the point of overflowing. Streets and squares are packed with people and there are not enough moorings in the port. You have to wait hours while the beaches absorb the excess of passers-by to calmly take in what is possible the rest of the year: the serenity of an old city, with a great deal of history in its streets and in the public's memory.

It is easy to trace the layout of the old walls in the arch that currently charts three consecutive passages (Constitució, Jaume I and Capità Negrete) and which is popularly known as **Sa Contramurada**. It is contained by two imposing bastions, one of which is crowned by the Town Hall —previously a citadel, during Muslim rule— while the other houses are dominated by the **Bastió de sa Font Museum** (see p. 190-191). They overlook the port and its extension, the **Pla de**

In summer the port is a setting of continuous movement

Ses Voltes, the backbone of the old city

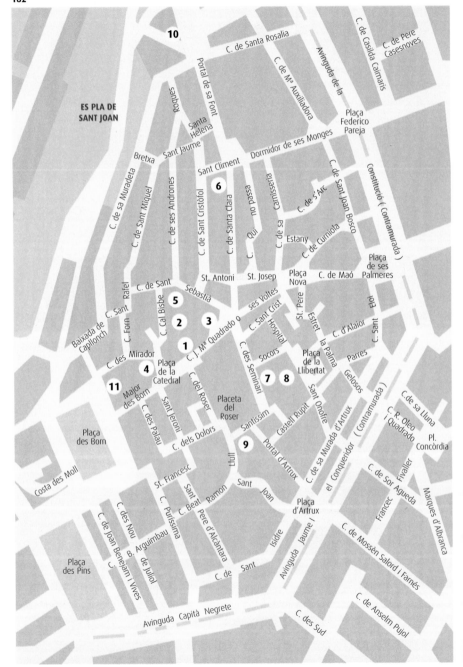

10

ES PLA DE SANT JOAN

C. de Santa Rosalia

C. de Mª Auxiliadora

Avinguda de la

C. de Casilda Caimaris

C. de Pere Casesnoves

Roqueta

Portal de sa Font

Santa Helena

Sant Jaume

Bretxa

C. de sa Muradeta

C. de Sant Miquel

C. de ses Andrones

C. de Sant Cristòfol

C. de Santa Clara

Sant Climent

Dormidor de ses Monges

Plaça Federico Pareja

Carnisseria

C. de Sant Joan Bosco

Constitució (Contramurada)

6

C. de s'Arc

Qui no passa

C. de sa

Estany

C. de Curniola

Plaça de ses Palmeres

St. Antoni

St. Josep

Plaça Nova

C. de Maó

C. de Sant

Sebastià

C. Cal Bisbe

C. Forn Rafel

Baixada de Capllonch

C. Sant

5

2

3

M ̊ Quadrado

ses Voltes

C. Sant Crist

St. Pere

Estret

Eloi

C. d'Alaior

C. Sant

1

C. J.

Hospital

la Palma

Parres

C. des Mirador

4

Plaça de la Catedral

C. del Roser

C. des Seminari

Socors

7 **8**

Plaça de la Llibertat

Geloses

11

Major des Born

Sant Jeroni

C. des Palau

Placeta del Roser

Santíssim

Castell Rupit

Sant Onofre

C. de sa Murada d'Artrux

el Conqueridor (Contramurada)

C. de sa Lluna

C. R. Oleo i Quadrado

Pl. Concòrdia

Plaça des Born

C. dels Dolors

9

Ltull

Portal d'Artrux

Costa des Moll

St. Francesc

C. des Nou

C. de Joan Benejam i Vives

C. de Juliol

B. Arguimbau

Puríssima

Sant Pere d'Alcàntara

Beat Ramon

Sant

Joan

Plaça d'Artrux

C. de Sor Agueda

Francesc

Fivaller

Marques d'Albranca

Plaça des Pins

C. de

Sant

Isidre

Avinguda Jaume I

C. de Mossèn Salord i Farnés

C. de Anselm Pujol

Avinguda Capità Negrete

C. des Sud

Sant Joan, the setting for the equestrian games held during the festivals (see p. 188-189).

The medieval city, within these limits, holds many interesting buildings. Its backbone goes from Plaça Alfons III to **es Born**. Until reaching the **Plaça Nova** it goes under the name of Camí de Maó, like the old entrance road to the city, today replaced by the main road. Later it becomes **Ses Voltes** (Carrer Josep M. Quadrado), whose narrow road runs between the vaulted porches of the houses.

The harmonious succession of arches is only broken by the short extension of the **Plaça Vella**, where one can see a bronze representation of the emblematic **Be de Sant Joan** (St. John's lamb), a delicate sculpture by Quetglas. This is behind the cathedral church, a building where religious belief and citizen's awareness converge, as a real and symbolic centre of this area.

Without being taller than other urban buildings, that of the **Seu** (See) impresses the observer due to its position and because it rises dramatically among the empty spaces surrounding it. The church of Santa Maria was built in the 14th century on the site of the old Muslim mosque, which had already been adapted to Christian worship since the arrival on the island of Alfons III; it was consecrated as a cathedral in 1795. Built according to the patterns of Catalan Gothic, it is made up of a single and wide nave, joined by several side chapels. It has been repaired and rebuilt so many times that it is no won-

der that there are Baroque elements present, such as the chapel of **Ses Ànimes**, or neo-classical ones, such as the main façade. As the city's main worshipping centre, it has experienced its happier moments as well as suffered its tragedies. The Turkish hordes of the pashas Mustafa and Piali looted and pillaged the city in 1558, *s'any de sa desgràcia*, (the tragic year), setting fire to the area.

The **Palau Olivar** also stands in the Pla de la Seu and its projecting facade seems to guard over the logical way forward towards **Es Born**. It is nevertheless a good idea to delay the march forward and take time to get lost among the neighbouring little streets. In Carrer del Bisbe is the Episcopal Palace,

Molí des Comte, in Plaça Alfons III

and in the adjoining Carrer Sant Sebastiá the **Palau Squella**, a Baroque building of 18th century Italian style. Further on, in Carrer Santa Clara, is the **Palau Baró de Lloriac**, the oldest family name of the local noblesse, forming a corner with Carrer Dormidor de ses Monges, where stands the convent of the nuns of the Order of St. Clare, so closely linked to the vicissitudes of the city. Going back towards Ses Voltes along the same street, you pass between the small church of Sant Josep and **Can Salord**, with the corner set back, surely for easing the entry and exit from the church.

On crossing **Ses Voltes**, a victim of the never-ending flow of pedestrians that pass up and down, the street takes the name of Bisbe Vila, but the **Carrer del Seminari** is more popular because here is the Augustine convent of **Socors**, in Renaissance style and headquarters of the council seminary. The cloister plays host to the Music Festival on summer nights as well as auditions for the **Capella Davídica**, an institution that has cultivated many famous and appreciated voices. Before, however, you will have passed in front of another small chapel, that of Sant Crist, and another palace, that of the second branch of the Saura dynasty, today occupied by bank offices.

Behind the convent of Socors is a space with a life of its own: the market, in the **Plaça de la Llibertat**, with an architectural style —in iron, supplied by the Modernists— that provides a great leap of two centuries in the area's appearance, although possessing the character necessary for it not to be too striking a difference.

There are more palaces in **Carrer del Santíssim**, those of **Saura** and **Martorell**, and the **church of Roser** —secularised and used as a cultural centre—, and more small, narrow streets which give off a feeling of intimacy and peace. This continues until leaving the Born area, where the **Salord and Olivar** mansions, by now 19th century buildings, sublimate the representative intention of these dwellings —the stately houses or palaces—, whose façades often provide a more spectacular architectural style.

The **obelisk of Born** can be seen as an index finger accusing, as an accusation to the heavenly powers for the abandonment suffered when faced with calamity. The monument, however, a homage to the victims of the Turkish attack, must also be interpreted as confirmation of nobility which it does not renounce. **Ciutadella de**

Menorca is very aware of its past and the role it has had to play has not always been a kind one. The fact that the British occupation took away its character of capital, for example, has not prevented it from preserving the pride with which it bore this title.

Facing the palaces already mentioned is the Town Hall, and to the side, the **Teatre des Born**, alongside which the port can be reached via the steps of the Baixada Capllonch. Another way is through the Costa des Moll, which opens out between this square and the adjoining **Esplanada des Pins**, another setting of urban peace. If instead of going down to the port, you go along the Passeig de Sant Nicolau, you reach the entrance to the open sea and the Passeig Marítim which follows the line of Cala Degollador. In the **Plaça Almirall Farragut** —an illustrious American sailor of local descent— stands the **Sant Nicolau Castle**, an elegant military construction from which an additional turret stands out for guard duty. Octagonal in design, and surrounded by a moat, it possessed the artillery required for repelling attacks from sea. It was planned by Spanish engineers at the end of the 17th century to replace another, from which the coat of arms it bears came from, that of the Aragonese Crown.

The spirit of summer materialises each year in Ciutadella with the arrival of the **Sant Joan** festivals, revealing the Mediterranean heart that beats beneath its venerable exterior. This spirit does not rest until the days become shorter again. The nights must be filled with people and music as much as possible, dispelling the austere fame of being a city of convents.

SANT JOAN FESTIVALS

Ciutadella is synonymous with **St John**, with the **festivals**. Many people associate these festivals with the image of those magnificent horses elevated amongst the crowd, the raucous sounds of the music, the almond shells turned into small missiles or the daily ablutions with gin. There is a great deal of cheer, a great deal of energy, as well as respect to signs of identity and great fervour. Its protagonists jealously watch over the festivals in order to maintain their original meaning and reverential liturgy.

The horses rise up on their rear legs amidst the mass of people

The **caixers**, members of the brotherhood, dress in the clothing that their predecessors wore: white trousers and shirt, bow tie, boots with spurs and tail coat. They also carry a small whip and cover themselves with the *guindola*, a bicorne hat that gives them poise and identifies them as repositories of a secular tradition. They faithfully follow the rules of medieval origins that ascribe a very specific representation to the distinct historical social classes: the peasantry, the nobility, and the clergy...

The events begin on the Sunday before the 24th of June, **diumenge des Be,** or Lamb Sunday, when a beautiful lamb is walked around the streets of the city, the culminating moment arriving on the evening before and during the saint's day, when the *caixers* ride around the old quarter on horseback. The **fabioler**, playing his small flute, heads the **qualcada** (the procession) on a donkey. The **caragols** take place (the spiralling turns they make) with the repeated game of demanding that the jockeys ride their mounts reared up, in a rampant attitude, which is called **fer un bot** (rising up), and the frenzy continues through to the following day, when different equestrian events are held in the Pla de Sant Joan: *ensortilles, ses carotes, correr abraçats...* For two days the city throbs unceasingly.

One of the competitions held in the Pla de Sant Joan

BASTIÓ DE SA FONT MUSEUM

The Sa Font bastion was one of the improvements made in fortifying the city in the 17th century. It survived the demolition work that would later open up the old quarter to the extramural extensions and has had several uses since those times. This building supplied light (acetylene street lighting) and water (due to its large water tank). It is now a source from which culture springs, in the widest sense of the word: as impressive inside as it is on the outside, the bastion is the perfect setting for the items housed in the museum (which will be moved to the **Palau Saura** when it has been fully fitted out, the space being given over to the town's art schools). Its dynamic exhibition provides a historical and anthropological description of Ciutadella's past. Of exceptional quality and great scientific value are the series of objects recently discovered in the caves of **Càrritx** and **Mussol**.

10

BASTIÓ DE SA FONT
Ciutadella
Plaça de sa Font, s/n
Tel. 971 38 02 97

Archaeological pieces in one of the museum's vaulted rooms

AROUND CIUTADELLA

MAIN COVES AND BEACHES

The westernmost part of Menorca, coinciding with the part that forms the district of Ciutadella, is the driest part and most lacking in vegetation. It is only on its borders where the great green mass of **La Vall** appears, to the north, and the beginning of the ravine area to the south. Nor is it a land of dramatic slopes, but rather a large platform that progressively descends to the more southerly waters.

Cala d'Algaiarens
See pages 62-63

The most interesting points of scenic value are to be found along the coast, whereas inland provides the incentive to see varied examples of prehistoric remains and, in terms of rural architecture, some *cases de senyors*, stately homes, bearing witness to the bygone age of splendour, and the *barraques*, that are still standing on some estates. These constructions, refuges for sheep and pigs —although they seem like primitive temples, to be included in a list of prehistoric sites—, give credit to a certain skill in the use of stone that is to be admired.

Son Saura
Veure pàgina 64-65

From Ciutadella, the road network is extended like the sprawling legs of a spider. To the north east, the road leading to **Cala Morell** or **La Vall** passes in front of Torre d'en Quart, one of the buildings that include defence bastions (in the south, the same can be found in Torre Saura Vell). Towards the north-west, going towards **Punta Nati** (Cf-5) a rocky, arid landscape is crossed, impressive, however, for its selfsame toughness. Shortly before reaching the lighthouse, in the area that is Salamó, you can see an interesting *barraca* consisting of seven parts (photo on page 209).

Es Talaier
See pages 64-65

Towards the south, the Me-24 runs parallel to the east coast. This road leads to both **Santandria** and **Cala Blanca**, but continues on to **Cap d'Artrutx**, whose lighthouse ensures, with that of Capdepera, in Mallorca, navigation along the "canal" between the islands. The road continues until the developments of **Cala en Bosc** and **Son Xoriguer**. From the latter **Es Talaier** can be reached on foot, but it is a better idea to take a short cut in the direction of the beaches of **Son Saura** along the section of the Old Sant Joan Way that passes in front of **Son Catlar** (providing the opportunity to visit the archaeological dig). The other "unspoilt beaches", those of **Cala en Turqueta**, **Macarella** and **Macarelleta**, can be reached from other turnings off this Camí

Cala en Turqueta
See pages 66-67

Macarella and Macarelleta
See pages 68-69

Vell (Old Way), beyond the hermitage of **Sant Joan de Missa**, another example of rural architecture that is exquisite in its simplicity and which possesses great sentimental and symbolic value in local history. This is where the *caixers*, the members of the brotherhood, hold the religious services before the festivals.

The other beaches, closer to the western city, and therefore more rapidly filled, **Cala en Blanes**, **Cala en Brut**, **Cala en Forcat**, **Cales Piques**… do not have the same scenic value as those previously described, but are still interesting and have all kinds of services available.

The unmistakable character of Ciutadella de Menorca as a historic city surpasses its value as a central point for reaching the whole area. Due to its particularly Mediterranean character and the atmosphere that you can feel in its streets in chiaroscuro —with simple houses between which churches and stately homes are embedded—, for its port with a bridge and its very own atmosphere, it should be given special attention and the necessary time. You should also not forget

Punta Nati

that any trip made on the main road makes the archaeological digs of **Torre Trencada**, **Torre Llafuda** and the ***Naveta* des Tudons**.

Naveta des Tudons

A short distance from Ciutadella and right beside the main road —making it impossible to miss— stands this unique and spectacular megalithic construction. It was used as a collective burial chamber (able to contain one hundred bodies) and an ossuary, and its size is irrefutable proof of the importance given by its constructors to the rituals relating to life and death. You can visit the inside, where the space is divided into two overlapping areas that appear after the entrance corridor or anteroom. Dated around 1400 BC, it is clearly pre-Talayotic, from the beginning of the Bronze Age.

The large blocks of stone used gave rise to the local legend that told of the work of giants (confronted, as is de rigour in these tales, by a maiden).

Naveta des Tudons, an incredible vestige of the prehistoric world

Torre Llafuda

This settlement, very nearby the previously mentioned one, can be reached by taking the turning on kilometre 37 of the main road. This time the area that habitually surrounds the *taules* is more clearly defined. There are also rounded dwellings and some caves, as well as the customary massive talayot. The *taula*, in contrast, is not very big, but half-hidden, its positioning amongst the trees gives it a special character, an enwrapped feeling that accentuates the magical atmosphere that is often attributed to these vestiges of ancient times.

Torre Trencada

The singular *taula* of this excavation is one of the most interesting, although none of the surrounding sanctuary area has been preserved. It has the peculiarity of having a third stone attached at the side to ensure its stability. Excavated burial grounds and a talayot can also be seen. There is a picnic area and a path, flanked by the wood that leaves the main road at kilometre 39.

Caves of Cala Morell

Some can be seen just on entering this urbanisation on the north coast, but you will have to take a left turn to reach the small ravine where the majority of them are situated. It might seem, due to the constructive work and the decorations in them, that their architects enjoyed living in them… but the remains found in them, and in others of a similar form, show that they were in fact a necropolis in the late Talayotic period and were not relatively comfortable dwellings. In several of these caves appear the so-called *capades de moro*, open oval-shaped cavities in the rocks that may have been niches for placing offerings or simple ossuaries.

There are also archaeological remains at the summit of the **Coll de Cala Morell**, the headland closing the cove on the east.

Taula de Torre Llafuda

This piece of the Son Catlar site was unable to remain standing

Open space of the megalithic wall of Son Catlar

Son Catlar

On the way to the beach of Son Saura it is a good idea to stop and visit this excavation for the variety of items that it holds, representative of a long period of occupation. For example, it is completely appropriate to talk about a megalithic construction when referring to the wall surrounding the Son Catlar settlement, since they are huge stones that make up this defence, but there are appendices in the form of towers that might confirm the use of settlements like this one during the period of Roman colonisation. The same occurs with the varied structure of the dwellings, although the central precinct of *taula*, hypostyle halls and the talayot on its north face clearly suggest its origin.

The caves of Cala Morell were used for burial purposes

Cala Morell

The same road leaves Ciutadella towards the north to reach this cove and, further on, that of **Algaiarens**. Around Cala Morell and within the same development, the variety of soils and rocky formations suggest to us that we are at the end of a geological fault separating the two geological origins of the Menorcan territory, with siliceous rocks in the north and calcareous rock in the south. Man's presence in this area goes back to prehistoric times, as shown by the previously described caves (see p. 196), but his greater influence today reduces the beach even further, already small, and many bathers share the jetties and platforms that can be made out from the cliffs to sunbathe on.

Cala en Forcat

The area between **Pont d'en Gil**, a spectacular natural arch cut back into the cliff, and the estuary of the port of Ciutadella, is the most densely urbanised part of the district. Its border to the north is the Torre del Ram hippodrome. Their uses for tourism dates back to the early days of the boom in the sector and includes different centres, among which some small coves remain almost hidden. The narrowness of these inlets is exaggerated by the height of the cliff, on which platforms have been built (the most typical one being in **Cala en Brut**) which aim to make up for the lack of real beach space.

Cala en Forcat looks southwards, "guarded" by a large hotel that leans over the water.

Cala Morell, sheltered by Punta de s'Elefant (on the left)
Cala en Forcat, hidden in an area that is highly populated during the summer

Cala en Blanes

The path following the north shoreline of the Port de Ciutadella has traditionally been one of the favourite routes of the local people, until reaching **Sa Farola**, the lighthouse that shows navigating boats the situation of the estuary. Extending the route a little more than a kilometre takes you to **Cala en Blanes**, which can also be reached by the outer road that connects the city with the urbanisation of the same name. Less narrow and with a more extended inlet than those previously mentioned, this cove also boasts of a small sandy area with palm trees at the back. It is a spot where you can also take some fresh air, or a fresh drink, or both, when the sun is no longer at its hottest. Worth remembering though, is that in summer these small coves, due to their closeness to Ciutadella, often hang up the "full" sign.

Santandria

The short distance separating Santandria from Ciutadella seems to get less and less as the route is gradually absorbed by the city, since the continuous addition of new chalets is turning the road into a street. The beach, with so much development around, has also become small in the eyes of the local people, though it maintains its character as the scenario for local leisure. A projection of coastline protects the estuary and shelters the tiny beach of **Sa Caleta**. Over this selfsame point is a defensive tower, **Es Castellar**, built in the 18th century as an attempt to stop ransacking by a possible invader after the experience of the French landing. There is a deep-sea diving centre and parasol and sun lounger rental. A curiosity is the presence of a freshwater spring.

Cala en Blanes, at the end of a long inlet of the sea
Santandria beach. On the right, the small Sa Caleta

Cala Blanca

Between the previous cove, Santandria, and this new cove open to the west, the urbanisations that take the name of one or the other are spread along the whole stretch facing the sea. This means that you can go from one to another along their streets, without returning to road from Artrutx. It is not surprising, therefore, that from so much space given over to tourist accommodation there are enough users to monopolise the use of the beach, or nearly enough.

Despite the competition, it is a good idea to keep this cove in mind due to its closeness to Ciutadella, for the usual quality of the water and sand, as its name insinuates, and for all the services available, including restaurants. There are interesting archaeological spots around too: several caves and remains of a *naveta*.

Cala en Bosc

The land drops gently down until submerging into the sea at **Cap d'Artrutx**, on the south-east side of the island. There is no interruption between the sector surrounding the lighthouse and which takes this name and the nearby development, with hotels that have surrounded the Cala en Bosc beach and includes a sports port converted from the small marshy land that was once there. It is from this port that the boats leave to visit the coves in the southern part of the Ciutadella district.

The growth in the number of tourist places has brought with it the appearance of all kinds of complementary services, with special emphasis on water sports. Visitors can choose between navigating the seas, diving or flying on skis (parascending).

Cala Blanca beach
Cala en Bosc has become sandwiched between adjoining developments

After the fishing trip, the small boat returns to the shelter of a cove

Son Xoriguer

This beach is double the width of the neighbouring Cala en Bosc, from which it is separated by the Punta de sa Guarda, but by being more exposed to the open sea its strip of sand is comparatively thin, also showing the unguarded western sector with the rocky ground in sight. Behind both beaches, the developed area is continuous, just like that described between Santandria and Cala Blanca. It is the point where tourist developments stop as after this point come the protected areas, another reason why all the surface area available is taken up... reaching even as far as the old Camí de Cavalls path, which follows the coastline.

Son Xoriguer is the last sandy area before the "unspoilt beaches"

STONE AND QUARRIES

PEDRERES DE S'HOSTAL
Ciutadella
Camí vell, km 1
Tel. 971 48 15 78
www.lithica.es

In the past, the *marès*, sandstone, cut into ashlars was the most used construction material. This sandy stone —of marine origin as its name suggests— was extracted from the same land on which the houses were to be built, but the growing demand very soon justified the opening of quarries. Production is still maintained in some, but the majority of them were abandoned when lighter materials became available to use.

Today, a hard-working association, **Líthica**, is trying to recover and preserve these unique precincts open to the heavens. After cleaning up and converting the spaces into pleasant gardens, some, like the S'Hostal (in Ciutadella, see file), can already be visited, and prove to be an excellent setting for cultural and leisure events.

Like a "totem" of bygone times, the great cut out profile overlooks the quarry

In the countryside, there are still *barraques*, or huts, as impressive as this one

PRACTICAL
GUIDE

WALKS
HANDICRAFTS
GASTRONOMY
POPULAR FESTIVALS
CULTURE
NAUTICAL ACTIVITIES
CYCLE-TOURING
OTHER ACTIVITIES
ACCOMMODATION
TRANSPORT
ORGANISATIONS AND PUBLIC SERVICES
HEALTHCARE AREA

WALKS

SA MESQUIDA → ES GRAU

Interest: Scenery and walking
Approximate time: 3-4 h

Any time of year is good for walking around different parts of the island, but it is always recommendable to set off with suitable footwear, and with the head covered in summer. This route is quite long but easy for anyone used to walking. Before setting off from the beach to start the route, it is well worth stopping for a moment to take in **Sa Mesquida** from the headland where the defensive tower was built by the British at the end of the 18th century.

From the far end of Sa Raconada Vella, the small cove located behind the Pa Gros outcrop, we start walking north along the coastal path that takes us to **Es Grau** with the sea on our right. It is precisely in this seascape, which does not leave us throughout the excursion, where the main attraction of the walk lies, also offering an interesting perspective over this north coast near to Maó, rough and unspoilt despite being just around the corner.

The route follows a relatively high path except for two points where it drops to the sea, **Macar de Binillautí** and the **Caleta de Binillautí**. The last notable projecting piece of land is the **Punta de sa Galera**, from where the islets of Sa Cúdia can be made out already and which, along with **Illa d'en Colom**, mark out the maritime entrance to the Es Grau cove. From this point you can take a short cut through the streets of an unfinished urbanisation (it is possible to continue along the coastline but it will prolong our walk considerably).

In summer there are buses connecting the two beaches with Maó, but during the rest of the year you will have to ensure you have transport organised at the end of the walk. In Es Grau there are several restaurants and bars where you can relax taking in the beach and the setting of the Natural Park.

Cala des Tamarells

Cap de LLevant

Illa d'en Colom

Punta Fra Bernat

Platja des Grau

Illots de sa Cudia

ES GRAU

s'Albufera
Parc Natural

Punta de sa Cudia

sa Cudia Nova

Punta de sa Galera

s'Albufera

es Violar

sa Bassa

ses Salvatges Primes

Caló de ses Mandries

s'Albufera des Grau

Cala Grau

sa Cudia Vella

ses Salvatges Fondes

Caleta de Binillautí

es Planàs

ses Piquetes

GR 223

Macar de Binillautí
en Bombarda

Milà Nou

Milà Vell   Estància de Milà

Binillautí Nou

s' Esquena d'Ase

Binillautí Vell

es Milà

Binillautí

sa Raconada Vella

Milà   92

es Pa Gros
I. de sa Mesquida

Cala Mesquida

Torre de sa Mesquida

SA MESQUIDA   Alblauet   Punta de sa
Bateria Vella

N

Punta Negre

0   1
1 km

ES MURTAR

PUNTA PRIMA
→BARRANC DE RAFALET

Interest: Scenery and cultural
Approximate time: 2-3h

The first section of the walk is at sea level, following the coastline, which is low at this end of the island. You go west from the Punta Prima beach, with the Illa del Aire on the right and the Alcalfar tower as the first objective in sight. In a short while you encounter some saltworks built midway through the last century but were never finally used. Further on, the defence tower, restored and fitted out as an occasional hostel, more or less marks the half way mark of the route. Below you appears the small Caló Roig beach. From here the scenery changes, no longer arid because the first ravine is reached, the **Alcalfar** ravine, then the cove and holiday complex that goes by the same name. After the necessary break we must cross all of Alcalfar until reaching the road that leads to the Algar urbanisation.

At this point there are two possibilities: a very wide and short road that ends at the entrance to the **Pinaret de S'Algar** —a small pine wood where a camping area has been fitted out— and a dirt track that is suitable for vehicles. The latter is the one you should take. Passing the houses that appear on both sides you reach a point where a chain impedes vehicles from passing. Crossing the obstacle, the path enters an oak grove that covers the last section of the ravine. Here the trees have grown right up to the high part of the cleft, forming a canopy over the dry bed and giving us shade all along the path that ends in the small cove.

CAP DE SES PENYES

Interest: Scenic
Approximate time: 2 hours there and back

From the area close to the Paleochristian basilica or from before reaching Son Bou —also before the small tunnel on the road— you can walk to the very best viewpoint of the whole area. From the heights of **Cap de ses Penyes**, the destination point of the trip, we can see that the line of large sandy areas that go from Binigaus to Son Bou ends here, terminating the sequence of land that gently descends to the sea. From this point onwards, in an easterly direction, between the **Llucalari** and Cala en Porter ravines appears a large plateaued area of a considerable height, lands facing the sea with the appearance of a natural fortress. They drop sharply, with numerous caves in the cliffs, and are relatively unspoilt due to the fact that for many years these parts were within a militarily controlled area.

More interesting than the path we have taken is the series of views from this unique spot. The closest ravine, down to the **Llucalari cove** (if you have time and the weather permits, you can go down to it for a swim) is great, but the magnificence of the view multiplies when we look west, with the straight sandy area of Son Bou below us, marking the border between the immense sea and the **Es Prat** wetland, where the **Son Boter** and **Es Bec** ravines flow out. On this headland, a magnificent grandstand to see the sun setting behind neighbouring Mallorca, the more hidden side of the island impresses us more forcefully, precisely when behind us we confront an infinite horizon of unreachable proportions.

Cala de Llucalari

Sant Jaume Mediterrani

Son Bou

Sant Jaume

Son Bou

Llucalari

Estància d'en Carreres

Platges de Son Bou

Llucalari Nou

Llucalari de Sant Antoni

Basílica de Son Bou

Sant Llorenç

Barranc de Torre Vella

Torre Vella

Cap de ses Penyes

Caleta de Llucalari

N

1 km

Cova de sa Calç

El Cap de Ses Penyes

PLATJA DE CAVALLERIA → BINIMEL·LÀ

Interest: Scenic
Approximate time: Over 2-hours

Another coastal walk, which this time goes between two undeveloped beaches on the north coast and enables you to see how the sea has eroded the coastline, with its successive outcrops, reefs, small beaches and *macars*, or pebbles (where large stones, *macs*, replace the sand), providing the observer with a sample of not curious images. Geology enthusiasts will be delighted by the variety of soils we find along the way, but the scenery we see is gratifying in itself.

As in other cases, you should plan where the pick-up point should be since this is a long walk and may tire out anyone who is not in the best of form. The walk can also be divided into two parts —for two different days— arriving only at the **Cala Mica** midway, from either end of the itinerary. Doing this walk in the middle of summer allows you to have a refreshing swim in the sea at the midway point before setting off to finish. You will run the risk of sunburn, however, if you do not take a hat with you; there is no vegetation to provide us with shade.

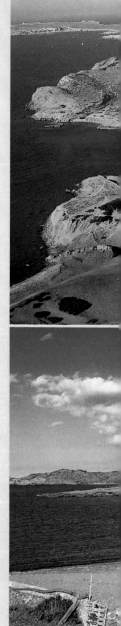

Cala Mica

Platja de Cavalleria

ES MIGJORN
→ COVA DES COLOMS

Interest: Scenery and cultural
Approximate time: 3-4 h

From inland to the sea, the route for this trip is always in a descendant direction, which means that it is by no means tiring, even in summer. It starts in the town itself, along the path that leaves the old cemetery. You should look out for the red arrows that now and again mark the way, since even though it drops down the right side of the ravine, it must be first crossed in order to reach this interesting spot.

The **Cova des Coloms** is a very wide cavity, with a high vaulted ceiling, giving it its deserved nickname of "the Cathedral". Its impressive size is even more startling since you get no idea of the dimensions until the moment you reach the threshold as the leafy fronds of a fig tree keep the entrance half hidden.

A short distance further on are other caves, such as **Na Polida**, interesting for the profusion of stalagmites and stalactites that fill its chambers. Torches are required to visit it… and a great deal of care as well as the company of an expert if possible, along with the utmost respect for the chambers and their contents, given their already fragile state.

In the heading we have placed the cave as the main objective, but the logical continuation of our walk consist of going down to the beaches of **Binigaus** (though there is always the option of going back). On reaching the sea, you must continue walking eastwards until reaching the Santo Tomàs beach, where you will have arranged the pick-up point in car or the use of public transport for returning to Es Migjorn.

Sant Roc

Font Redona de Baix

sa Canaleta

Albranca Vell

Torre

Me-20

Sant Josep

Albranxella

ES MIGJORN GRAN

Son Carabassa

de

Binicodrell Nou

Son Pons

Binicodrell

Sant Miquel

sa

Torre Vella

Estància Cornabou

s'Alzinar

na Llarga

sa Quintana

Binigaus Vell

Santa Clara

Binigaus

Santa Mònica

Santa Mònica

Barranc

de

Torre Nova

Binigaus Nou

Me-18

sa Teulera

Cova des Coloms

Sant Agustí

Son Saura

Binicodrell de Baix

Barranc

de

Sant Agustí

Cova de na Polida

Sant Adeodat

Son Pinaret

Torrent de Son Boter

Sant Tomàs

ses Cuques

sa Vall

Punta de na Rabiosa

Platges de Binigaus

Escull Codrell

Platja de Sant Adeodat

Punta Negra

SANT TOMÀS

Platja de Sant Tomàs

Punta de Talis

Talis

Punta Rodona

Platges de Son Bou

0   N   1

1 km

CASTELL DE SANTA ÀGUEDA

Interest: Scenic and cultural
Approximate time: 2h 30m

This is a trip, or stroll, that takes us to a height of 264m, allowing you to take in the extensive views across the area. Although the ruins of the old fortress are crying out to be preserved, it is well worth visiting it for several reasons. These are the route itself, which takes us to the summit along a paved Roman-style road, the scenery of the oak grove during the climb and that which it overlooks upon reaching the top; and the presence of some vestiges of Muslim origin, the least represented on the island if we discount the place names (for example, in the names beginning with *al* or *bini*).

The Islamic domain lasted longer in Menorca than on the Iberian Peninsula due to the agreements reached between their *almosharifs*, or tax and rent inspectors, and the Christian forces. The governors had their summer residence on this summit —with a more pleasant temperature than on the coast— and while they could relax looking out over their possessions, a walled precinct protected them and any attempt to lay siege on them would be easily spotted. The last occupant to enjoy this post was the *valí* or governor, Said ben Haham.

The Catalan conquest saw the installation here of a governor of a large district, **Santa Àgueda**, which covered the territory that is today shared between Ferreries, Es Migjorn and Es Mercadal. A small community settled around the fortress and a chapel was devoted to the saint that still today bears the name of the spot.

This period came to a close in the mid-14th century with its abandonment, and although it had diverse uses, its decline and deterioration could not be avoided. It is still however a place of great interest for its design and the other reasons mentioned, and because, by placing ourselves above the most frequented spots, it makes us reflect about the use now being made of them.

Castell de Santa Àgueda

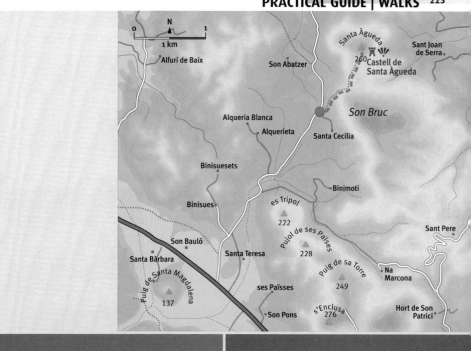

- Alfurí de Baix
- Son Abatzer
- Santa Àgueda
- Sant Joan de Serra
- 260 Castell de Santa Àgueda
- *Son Bruc*
- Alqueria Blanca
- Alquerieta
- Santa Cecília
- Binisusets
- Binimoti
- Binisues
- es Tripol
- 222
- Pujol de ses Països
- 228
- Sant Pere
- Son Bauló
- Santa Teresa
- Santa Bàrbara
- Puig de sa Torre
- 249
- Na Marcona
- Puig de Santa Magdalena
- 137
- ses Països
- Son Pons
- s'Enclusa 276
- Hort de Son Patrici

N

0   1 km

HANDICRAFTS

Traditional handicrafts have been kept alive by the expert hands of some experienced people who have worked hard to continue them and hand down their skills to others. Mechanisation reached the costume jewellery and footwear trades a long time ago and now they are industries (although they continue to incorporate a great deal of manual work). On the other hand, many articles of wickerwork, pottery and other handmade goods are not given the use they were invented for... but, nevertheless, arouse great interest today for their efficient design, for having been saved from the passing of time... and for the fact that they are handmade.

Experienced hands transform the wicker into baskets

You can find some interesting pieces of kiln-fired pottery in Menorca, unglazed and barely refined, which covered different needs in bygone times. Pitchers are still made (*de barca*, *de cul estret* —narrow-necked—, castanyes), bottles (the *buldrofa* or ses *botilles*), clay pipes with a wooden bit —the farm workers used them to smoke *pota*, a rough tobacco substitute—, buckets (the *caduf*, scoop used in wells), bowls (*ribelles*), demijohns (the *maridet* or bed-warmer for the sheets), watering cans, feeding troughs and "nests" for the farm animals.

La Gerreria d'en Artur Gener, in Carrer Curniola 12, in Ciutadella, carries on the tradition and family techniques. In Maó, in Moll de Ponent 10, the Hermanos Lora Buzón company extends the traditional pieces on sale with contemporary work of their own, as well as publicly exhibiting the pottery and painting work. As is common in this field, where there are many more shops selling traditional or contemporary pottery, there are also many shops where you can find the popular **avarques**, country sandals (see next page), but if you want personalised dealings with the craftsman responsible you should go to Ca'n Doblas, in Plaça Jaume II in Ferreries.

In Es Mercadal is the **Centre Artesanal** (craft centre) of Menorca, where we can se an interesting display of distinct specialities (Tel. 971 15 44 36 | www.artesaniademenorca.com) and in the different towns the antique and restorers' shops abound. This is not surprising, given the fact that the area has been nourished by a range of varied cultural influences, and in which, from the archaeological findings (today protected from possible commercial exploitation) to those which are a product of nature (fossils, for example), there are a myriad of objects that may be classified as "antiques". British and French rule, specifically, left behind a legacy of typical day-to-day objects, among which features classical English furniture. The demand for it generated a big industry, with the Sheraton and Chippendale styles being sought after in particular. The items produced in noble woods —by hand, of course—, and which were mainly made for the palaces and stately homes, are the most sought-after today, though examples of more rustic-style furnishing is also high up on collectors' lists, since this genre, while using more basic materials, was inspired by the models in vogue at the time and produced some interesting results.

THE FOOTWEAR INDUSTRY

Hide tanning was always an important activity in the Balearics while the islands came under the influence of the Muslim world, and perhaps it was the seed that germinated the trades that later derived from it. In fact, footwear has contributed to the writing of Menorca's

Experienced craftsmen still work the *espart* as in the past

recent history. The process of industrialisation that took off in the last quarter of the 19th century did so precisely with the opening of two shoe factories in Ciutadella. Within a short period of time, nearly half the active population was employed in this sector. From that time on and until the arrival of tourism, it has been the number one export. Today, in a globalised market where fierce competition reigns, very good sales are still maintained thanks to the exquisite designs and know-how of the craftsmen involved, most of them coming from Ciutadella and Alaior. Brands such as Pons Quintana, from Alaior, Patricia, from Ciutadella, or Jaime Mascaró, from Ferreries, with its *Pretty Ballerinas*, are present in the main shop windows of the five continents. These high-quality shoes (and other leather goods) can be bought in the manufacturers' own shops on the industrial estates, and you can also order made-to-measure handmade pairs in some small factories. Compared to the more traditional production of the factories, emphasis should be made of the enormous success of simpler and more popular footwear: the unmistakable **avarques**, the uppers made of cow hide and the soles from tyres, one hundred per cent walker-friendly… and cosmopolitan since they attracted a young, urban following.

The *avarques*, country sandals, will soon become as universal as jeans

GASTRONOMY

**OUTSTANDING
RESTAURANTS**

MAÓ

Cap Roig
Cala Mesquida
Tel. 971 18 83 83
S'Espigó
Moll de Llevant, 267
Tel. 971 36 99 09
Es Fosquet
Moll de Llevant
Tel. 971 35 00 58
Aroma sensacions
Moll de Llevant, 314
Tel. 971 36 35 94
Es Molí de foc
Sant Llorenç, 65
(Sant Climent)
Tel. 971 15 32 22
Varadero
Moll de Llevant, 4
Tel. 971 35 20 74
Can Bernat des Grau
Road Maó-Fornells
km 3, Tel 650 974 685

ES CASTELL

Ca'n Delio
Cales Fonts
Tel. 971 35 17 11
España
Victory, 50
Tel. 971 36 32 99
Trébol
Cales Fonts, 43
Tel. 971 36 70 97
Vell Parrander
Cales Fonts, 52
Tel. 971 36 94 19

Menorcan cuisine is simple and adapts to the produce supplied by the land and sea at different times of the year. It can, therefore, assimilate concepts of both Mediterranean and market cuisine, but without forgetting that successive historical occupations have added recipes and methods that have given it some rather exotic nuances.

Inversely, the famous mayonnaise has gone round the world after its discovery here by the French, and lobster stew, the most asked-for dish, is also on the way to achieving international fame. In recent years the clientele has grown in restaurants that make an effort to promote part of the cultural heritage, showing that a simple oliaigo (tomato and vegetable soup) can win applause when made with love and devotion. This dish, served with figs when in season, is based on a lightly-fried mix of onion, garlic, green pepper and a lot of tomatoes and is served with slices of bread, forming a soup broth. Oven-baked dough provides a host of recipes, from the formatjades, melted cheese dishes, to the coques de tomàtiga, tomato-based pizza breads. Among the cured meats feature sobrassada, camot and carn i xua. The sea also boasts of its delights: escopinyes gravades (the common clam), dàtils (date mussels), corns (whelks)… and there are a wealth of sweet cakes and pastries: amargos, ensaïmades, crespells, pastissets…

To try fresh fish or stews you should preferably go to the "harbour" restaurants. Also recommendable are those that are dedicated to specialities of Menorcan cuisine and those in the country or on the outskirts of towns, in old houses, often with an outdoor dining area, where the setting is a pleasant complement to what is on offer on the menu. The following list is just an approximation of the more interesting restaurants.

As regards the wines, we must speak of a spectacular recovery of the sector. After having almost completely abandoned vine growing, there are now eight cellars that produce high-quality wines promoted under the label of **"Vi de la Terra Illa de Menorca"**. In Ciutadella we will come across **Vinyes Binitord** and **sa Marjaleta**, in Ferreries **Hort de Sant Patrici**, in Es Mercadal the **Ferrer de Montpalau** cellar, in Alaior **Vi de s'Illa S.L.**, in Maó **Vinya Sa Cudia**, with vineyards in the interior of the Natural Park of s'Albufera, and **Vins Solano**, in Sant Climent, and in Sant Lluís, finally, **Bodegas Binifadet**, which even produces an exceptional rosé cava.

And if progress is made producing wines, liqueurs also appear (in **Biniarbolla** they make the typical *herbes* and others of lemon or orange) and... beers. In Ciutadella, on the industrial estate **Illa** is manufactured; alongside the market, in Plaça de la Llibertat, **Sa Bona Birra** offers among many famous brands, their own traditionally made beer. Those produced in Sant Climent are also traditionally made: El Molí de Foc, Grahame Pearce and Sant Climent Lager.

Also returning is the production of oil by traditional methods, as is made in **Sa Tafona Nova**, an estate in Ciutadella, and in **Talatí de Baix**, an estate in Maó. What more can you ask for?

The traditional recipes still find old ovens that make them the best

SANT LLUÍS

La Caraba
S'Ullastrar, 78
Tel. 971 15 06 82
Son Ganxo
Passieg de sa Marina 66,
(Urb. Son Ganxo)
Tel. 971 15 90 75
Sa Pedrera des Pujol
Camí des Pujol, 14
(Caserío de Torret)
Tel. 971 15 07 17
Sa Parereta d'en Doro
Camí de Binisafuet, 75
Tel. 971 15 03 53

ES MERCADAL

N'Aguedet
Lepant, 30
Tel. 971 37 53 91
Molí des Racó
Carrer Major, 53
Tel. 971 37 53 92
Ca n'Olga
Pont de na Macarrana
Tel. 971 37 54 59
Tast
Pl. Pare Camps, 21
Tel. 971 37 55 87
Sol 32°
Pla de ses eres, 32
Tél. 971 15 42 06

FORNELLS

S'Àncora
Passeig Marítim, 7-8
Tel. 971 37 66 70
Es Cranc
Escoles, 31
Tel. 971 37 64 42
Es Pla
Passatge es Pla, s/n
Tel. 971 37 66 55
Es Cranc Pelut
Passeig Marítim, 98
Tel. 971 37 67 43
Sa Llagosta
Gabriel Gelabert, 12
Tel. 971 37 65 66

Ses Salines
Urb. Ses Salines
Tel. 971 37 67 45

ES MIGJORN GRAN

S'Engolidor
Carrer Major, 3
Tel. 971 37 01 93

FERRERIES

Es Barranc
Cala Galdana
Tel. 971 15 46 43
Binisues
Road Maó-Ciutadella,
km 31,6 (Camí d'Els
Alocs). Tel. 971 37 37 28
Liorna
Carrer de Dalt, 9
Tel. 971 37 39 12

CIUTADELLA

Cafe Balear
Pla de Sant Joan, 15
Tel. 971 38 00 05
Restaurant des Port
Marina, 23
Tel. 971 48 00 22
Ca's Ferrer
Portal de sa Font, 16
Tel. 971 48 07 84
El Bribón
Marina, 107
Tel. 971 38 50 50
La Payesa
Marina, 65
Tel. 971 38 00 21
Cas Cònsol
Plaça des Born, 17
Tel. 971 48 46 54
Es Tastet
Carnisseria, 9
Tel. 971 38 47 97
Smoix
Sant Isidre, 33
Tel. 971 48 05 16

LOBSTER STEW (*CALDERETA DE LLAGOSTA*)

The spiny lobster stew is the most known speciality, which everyone will mention as the glorious finishing touch after an unforgettable stay. A tasty delight that grows bigger in our memories due to the accompanied obligatory ritual of booking a table —if in the middle of August— and the scenery that gives it even more substance. More often than not, this added scenery is that of Fornells, because it was here where they soon realised that the dish would become an important source of income.

Before becoming the food of kings it was the prize the fishermen awarded themselves on the boat that provided their village with the succulent crustacean. Simple in elaboration and simple in seasoning, the dish hides no secrets apart form its main luxury ingredient (preferably a female spiny lobster) and the accompaniment of local produce (the tomatoes called *ferro*, iron, which are also the star turn of another popular Menorcan dish, the humble *oliaigo*, a tomato soup with garlic). As regards utensils, the earthenware pot is essential for serving it with fine slices of toasted bread (traditionally dry bread when eaten at home).

The massive demand has tripled the number of restaurants in For-

Lobster stew is the star dish of many restaurants

nells that specialise in these dishes, but it can be served up and tasted in good restaurants all over the island with the fullest guarantee. Another factor is that this demand has risen above the recommendable level of spiny lobsters caught and you may find the dish marked off the menu. In which case you will have to opt for the fish, seafood and lobster stews free of prejudice, which in the right hands reach similarly illustrious levels. If, however, it is on the menu: enjoy!

CHEESE

Menorcan cheese is generally known as "Maó" cheese, despite the fact that it is produced throughout the island. This is down to the fact that it was traditionally sold in the island's main port. Its characteristics and presentation have hardly changed since then either. The whole cheeses, square with rounded edges, show the marks of the canvases they were traditionally wrapped up in. It has had a denomination of origin certificate since 1985, although its fame dates back to the Middle Ages, when the Catalan monarchs made sure there was always a ready supply in their larders. It can be bought mild, medium, matured or vintage matured, but any of its varieties will please the most discerning of palates. As well as being delicious on its own, it is also excellent with fresh fruit (grapes) or

Menorcan cheese is a delicacy in any of its varieties

crystallised fruit (quince jelly) and forms an integral part of the island's culinary specialities.

MENORCAN GIN

Gin must be the most popular souvenir for visitors to remind them of their stay here when they have already returned home, or as a gift to friends. This is down to the fact that its special aroma and taste spark off an immediate association with everything connected to Menorca. Gin production dates back to the time of the first British occupation, but the distilling of the juniper berries does not follow the pattern of English gins to the letter and the result is rather distinct, starting with the presentation itself (artfully noticeable by being bottled in reproductions of glazed pottery bottles).

The maturing stills, which can still be seen today in the workrooms of Xoriguer in the port of Maó, play a key role in the process. This brand has become very popular and also bottles a variety mixed with lemonade, lessening its high alcohol content and which is commonly drunk at the festivals held all over the island during the summer months (the famous *pomada* or "Menorca Moonshine"). Another popular gin drink is the *pellofa*, with a slice of lemon and a dash of soda.

Stills for producing gin, a typical Menorcan product

POPULAR FESTIVALS

The enthusiasm with which the towns celebrate their festivals soon spreads to the visitor who has the chance to see or take part in them. The most attended festivals are those taking place during the summer months and revolve around the horses and their riders, the caixers, who are always the stars of the event.

Throughout the year the festivals on the Christian calendar are celebrated: **Christmas**, **Easter** or **All Saints**... while the annual Carnival also has a big impact, with balls and parades of floats in nearly all the towns. In some of these festivals a glimpse can be had of the religious and secular traditions, as well oddities such as *matar bujots* (killing puppets) —with blunderbusses— which the people from Ciutadella do on **Easter Sunday**.

The ruckus of the festivals infects the whole town

There are also institutional or historical festivals, such as the **Diada de Sant Antoni** (St. Anthony's Day, the 17th of January, to honour the patron saint of Menorca and celebrate the conquest of the island by Alfons III) or the **Commemoration of the attack by the Turks** (the 9th of July, when Ciutadella remembers the tragic events of 1558,

For St. Anthony they light *festers*, bonfires, in Ciutadella

S'any de sa desgràcia, the tragic year). It is during the heat of summer, however, when things really get turned up during the festivals in honour of the "titleholder" saints of each town. At this time of year, the work in the country took on less urgency and the locals were able to take a rest and eat more, in terms of both quantity and quality. Today, in contrast, the period coincides with a greater flow of tourists and if it were not for the authenticity transmitted by the local celebration, the festivals would appear to be merely massively attended events in which the main aspect was simply the spectacle.

CIUTADELLA

The Festival of **Sant Joan** (St. John) marks the beginning of all the summer festivals. On the Sunday before the 24th of June, a young farmer is given the task of announcing the oncoming festival, holding the most beautiful lamb in the district on his shoulders, with its combed fleece decorated with coloured ribbons. A musician accompanies him, the *fabioler*, who with his tabor and small flute marks the rhythm of all the events taking place from that moment on.

ES MERCADAL

The baton is handed over to this town during the third weekend of July, paying homage to **St. Martin**.

ES CASTELL

The festival takes place during the 24th, 25th and 26th of July in honour of the patron saint, **St. James**. Just like all the other festivals outlined in this section, the typical *jaleo*, or ruckus, is the most well attended event.

FORNELLS

The people of Fornells celebrate **St. Anthony** as a separate event to that held in Es Mercadal (the district to which it belongs administratively) during the fourth weekend of July.

ES MIGJORN GRAN

The festivals held in this town are the last of July (on the fifth weekend if there is one). Otherwise they are passed on to the first weekend in August should they coincide with others on the calendar. They are in honour of **St. Christopher**.

LLUCMASSANES

Even though this is a smaller town —it forms part of Maó— it has its own festival programme. It is held in honour of **St. Gaietà** on the first weekend of August.

ALAIOR

The denseness and flow of people to the festivals, in honour of **St. Lawrence**, are related to the growing importance of the town. It takes place in the first weekend after the 10th of August.

SANT CLIMENT

It is in a similar situation to Llucmassanes, but a long-standing tradition has established the festivals as "official" (there are also urbanisations that organise their own festivals but are excluded from the official calendar). During the third weekend of August.

FERRERIES

St. Bartholomew's Festival on the 23rd, 24th and 25th of August.

SANT LLUÍS

In honour of the saint to which the town is named after and during the last weekend of August.

The songs and dances of yesteryear enliven any celebration

MAÓ

The last local festivals have a very wide-ranging programme, but here also special emphasis is laid on the events starring the horses. These are the festivals in honour of the **Verge de Gràcia**, patron saint of the town, and the main celebratory days are the 7th and 8th of September.

The festival season with the participation of the horse-riders closes on the 10th of September, they are the festivals of **St. Nicholas** and the setting is the summit of El Toro. Another popular summer festival is on July the 16th in honour of the **Virgin of Carme**, patron saint of the seafaring people, with sea-going processions in the ports of Maó, Fornells and Ciutadella, where the Virgin is paraded and accompanied by decorated boats. Also related to the world of fishermen is the festival in honour of **St. Peter** on the 29th of June. By far the most attractive is the one held in the port of Maó with children's games organised.

CULTURE

A great many cultural events take place during the peak season months when a larger audience is guaranteed, and the effort made in organising the events is better compensated. Nevertheless, other events are held all year round because Menorcan society in general so demands it. For example, it is unthinkable that the long-standing of operatic concerts could be missed.

THEATRE

Over a quarter of a century of the prestigious **Es Born Theatre Prize** backs up the extensive and deep-rooted love of the theatre, which at the end of the 18th century, already produced figures such as **Joan Ramis i Ramis**, the author of notable neo-classical tragedies. Several local companies make up with great merit for the rare presence of foreign productions (due to the extra costs of producing on the island and the impossibility of venues with large capacities). Nevertheless, there are some who have encountered a new expressive space in the **Menorca Theatre Festival**, premiered at the end of 2000.

The **Teatre Principal** and **Orfeó Maonés**, in Maó, and the **Teatre Municipal** des Born, in Ciutadella, are the more common stage settings, but each town has their own, better or worse, because there are always enthusiastic local residents who want to put on a show.

JAZZ

In Spring the **Menorca Jazz Festival** takes place, with different venues each year. The **Jazz obert** association (www.jazzobert.com) is in charge of assuring the presence of top names who offers concerts in the **Claustre del Carme** within the capital's summer programme.

Moreover, there are the legendary jam sessions held in the **Casino de Sant Climent** on Tuesday evenings and sometimes on Thursdays.

CLASSICAL MUSIC

With a history that goes back over more than four decades, the **Summer Music Festival of Ciutadella** (www.jjmmciutadella.com) is the longest-running festival on the island. Traditionally, the concerts (ten on average) are held in a very special setting, the **Auditori**

dels Socors, although sometimes they have been held in the **Líthica** quarries (www.lithica.es), a space with just as much atmosphere. July and August.

The magnificent organ of the parish church of **Santa Maria de Maó** provides internationally known interpreters the chance to play in the **Matins de l'orgue** every morning at 11 a.m. from Monday to Saturday (excluding public holidays). On Wednesdays at 8.30 p.m. small orchestras and choirs contribute to the melodious sounds for the evening **Concerts de nit**. All these events are held in July and August. Also taking place in these months —usually on Fridays at 9.30 p.m.— are the concerts organised by **JJMM** (Young Musicians) (www.menorcaweb.net/jmdemao) in the Claustre de Sant Francesc of Maó.

There are several local orchestral groups that ensure there are concerts throughout the year, especially around Christmas time.

OPERA

In November, several performances are organised by the **Friends of the Opera** group, an association that also provides the backing choir for the international stars appearing. The love of opera goes back to the 19th century (the Teatre Principal in Maó was opened in 1829, even before the famous Liceu of Barcelona), and has featured many great names from the world of opera, such as **Joan Pons** and the baritone **Lluís Sintes**. There are also many choral groups, the most well known one being the Capella Davídica.

CINEMA

The cinema clubs, the Ateneu in Maó and Es Born in Ciutadella, share a programme throughout the year that satisfies film buffs. In summer, as well the commercial cinemas, there is a possibility to see open-air films at the Cinema a la fresca sessions in public squares. Also starting up is the **Mèdit**, a promising Mediterranean Film Festival in Ciutadella (www.medit.es).

MUSEUMS AND ART GALLERIES

The Menorcan people are also lovers of the plastic arts. From the interesting period at the end of the 18th century, that gave rise to artists such as Chiesa, father and son, or Calbó, until the present, where the work of Quetglas honourably stands out, for example, there has been no lack of well-known figures. On the list included below are several art galleries, both privately and publicly owned, since the function of the museums perfectly complements exhibitions of the most varied tendencies, showing that a rich period in ideas is currently being experienced and that new values are constantly appearing. As regards the museums, as well as those that have had extensive coverage on previous pages, there are others of equal interest —not all of them are devoted to plastic arts— and spaces of a diverse nature that provide visitors with historical information or collections with an ethnological value. More exhaustive information, with timetables and prices, can be found in the *Consell Insular de Menorca* website: www.menorcamonumental.net

ALAIOR

San Diego Cultural Centre In the old church of the same name. c/ Banyer, s/n. Tel. 971 37 10 02.
Sala Municipal d'Art Temporary exhibitions. c/ Major, 11.
Galeria Arantza & Cia c/ des Forn, 9. Tel. 971 37 13 61

ES CASTELL

Military Museum of Menorca Historical military material in one of the old barracks of the Esplanada. All working days and the first Sunday in each month from 10 a.m. to 1 p.m. Tel. 971 36 21 00 www.museomilitarmenorca.com
Sant Felip Castle Road to Cala Sant Esteve. The remains of this military construction can be seen from June to September. Arrange visit calling tel. 971 36 21 00 | www.museomilitarmenorca.com
Fort Marlborough Cala Sant Esteve. Many details of 18th century civil and military customs are brought to life with the aid of modern technologies. Opening times: Tuesday to Saturday from 9 a.m. to 7.30 p.m. Sunday and Monday from 9 a.m. to 3 p.m. Tel. 971 36 04 62

CIUTADELLA

Ciutadella City Museum "Bastió de sa Font" Plaça de sa Font, s/n. History, archaeology and ethnology. Tel. 971 38 02 97 | www.ajciutadella.org

Diocesan Museum of Menorca c/ del Seminari, 7. Pere Daura collection of contemporary painting, gold and silversmithing and religious art, paintings from the 17th and 18th centuries and archaeological items. Open: from 10 a.m to 2 p.m.; Sundays and Mondays closed. Tel. 971 48 12 97

Sala Municipal El Roser c/ del Roser. Tel. 971 38 35 63

Sant Nicolau Castle Temporarily closed. Tel. 971 48 41 55

Galeria Retxa c/ Nou de Juliol, 37. Tel. 971 38 18 06 | www.galeriaretxa.com

Galeria Vidrart c/ Roser, 8. Tel. 971 38 58 51 | www.galeriavidrart.com

Casa-Museu Pintor Torrent c/ de Sant Rafael, 11. Open: from 11 a.m to 1 p.m and 7,30 to 9,30 p.m.; Sundays closed.
Tel. 626 558 126 | www.menorcaweb.net/pintortorrent

Pedreres de s'Hostal Run by **Líthica**, an association dedicated to the protection of stone quarries, this is an interesting ensemble of both the oldest and newest quarries just two km. from Ciutadella on the Camí Vell de Maó. Recommended itineraries are well signposted within the site. Tel. 971 48 15 78 | www.lithica.es

Sant Joan de Missa (hermitage) can be visited on Mondays from 4 to 7 p.m.

FERRERIES

Binisues Museum of Natural Sciences Road Maó-Ciutadella, km 31,6, in the detour of Camí dels Alocs. The extensive collection of the Carreras brothers merits a visit apart from what may coincide with the pleasure of the restaurant that the estate houses.
Tel 971 37 37 28 | www.binisues.com

MAÓ

Museum of Menorca c/ Dr. Guàrdia, s/n, in the old convent of Sant Francesc. Both the setting and the contents are of great interest. Unique items from all periods illustrate the changes and socio-cultural evolution of Menorca from prehistoric times to today. Tel. 971 35 09 55
http://dgcultur.caib.es/user/cultura/museus/museudemenorca/museudemenorca2.htm

Claustre del Carme Plaça Miranda s/n. Temporary exhibitions, variable opening times.

Hernández Sanz-Hernández Mora Museum Several rooms of the Claustre del Carme. Historical Menorcan library, plus furnishing and painting from the 18th, 19th and 20th centuries. Monday to Saturday from 10 a.m. to 1 p.m. Tel. 971 35 05 97

Museum of the Scientific, Literary and Artistic Society c/ Sa Rovellada de dalt, 25. Among other items, there is an interesting collection of algae and fossils. Monday to Saturday from 10 a.m. to 2 p.m. and 4 to 10 p.m. Tel. 971 36 05 53 | www.ateneumao.org

Sala de Cultura la Caixa c/ Nou, 25.

Sala de Cultura sa Nostra S'Arraval, 32 (old convent of Sant Antoni). Temporary exhibitions. Tel. 971 36 68 54

Municipal Cemetery Museum of Maó Funereal museum, naive paintings and many votive offerings. From 8 a.m. to 7 p.m., every day.

Galeria Artara c/ Rosari, 18. Tel. 971 35 29 12 | www.galeriaartara.com

Galeria Kroma c/ Anuncivay, 7. Tel. 971 35 08 04

La Mola Fortress Guided visit every day. Opening times: from 10 a.m. to 6 p.m. (May); from 10 a.m. to 8 p.m. (Juny-September); from 10 a.m. to 2 p.m. (October-April). To arrange group visits, call tel. 971 36 40 40 | www.fortalesalamola.com

Galeria Encant c/ Infanta, 20. Tel. 971 36 44 16 | www.encant.net

ES MERCADAL

Cap de Cavalleria Eco-Museum Sa Nitja. Although currently lacking an exhibition space, the archaeological activities of the entity continue being developed. Tel. 971 35 99 99 | www.ecomuseodecavalleria.com

Fornells defence tower Exhibition: "The defence of an island". Open: from 10 a.m. to 2 p.m during the summer months. Closed Tuesdays.

Centre Artesanal de Menorca An opportunity to see together the work of the majority of the island's craftspeople and buy their pieces. Tel. 971 15 44 36 | www.artesaniademenorca.com

ES MIGJORN GRAN

Galeria Es Migjorn Gran c/ Sant Llorenç, 12. Open only from April to October. Watercolours with a Menorcan theme by Graham Byfield.

SANT LLUÍS

Ethnological Museum Es Cós, 4. The biggest and most spectacular mill, completely restored, houses a small museum containing an attractive collection of old tools and utensils. Tel. 971 15 10 84

NAUTICAL ACTIVITIES

Following the coastline is a constant source of beautiful images and surprises. In fact, many Menorcan people use up their annual holidays to make a tour of the island in their own *llaüt*, or catboat, the island's most popular craft. They may be rented if you are only on a short stay or just let yourself be taken peacefully around on those based in the two main ports and which operate in the surrounding area.

Important regattas use the island as a starting or finishing point

Bay of Fornells: a perfect setting for windsurfing

SEAFARING TRIPS

In the chapter on Port de Maó (see p. 105) we have already mentioned the possible excursions. There are three pleasure boats that leave from Port de Ciutadella and make trips —from 10 a.m. to 5 p.m.— to the beaches of Son Saura, Turqueta, Macarella and even Cala Galdana. They are called the **San Telmo II** and **Jumbo**, of the Menorca Blava (tel. 619 68 00 72 | www.menorcablava.com), and the **Fiesta**, owned by R. M. De la Cruz. Only from May to October (tel. 971 35 07 78 | www.rutasmaritimasdelacruz.com).

From **Cala en Bosc**, the **Amigos** boat, of Darío Pons, runs trips to Trebalúger and Escorxada, (tel. 618 34 80 06) and the **Don Pancho** does a similar itinerary.

Vintage offers catamaran departures from the port of **Ciutadella** to enjoy the sunsets (tel. 652 03 36 56, www.efvintage.com).

SAILING

Windsurf boards, sailboats and catamarans can be rented at **Wind Fornells**, on the small beach at Ses Salines in Fornells (they also organise courses: Tel. 664 33 58 01 | www.windfornells.com), at **Surf and Sail Menorca** in Son Xoriguer, (tel. 629 74 99 44 | www.surfsailmenorca.com), and on the majority of beaches with services. Longer boats can be rented at:

Menorca Cruising School
Moll de Llevant, 303 | Maó
Tel. 660 64 78 45 | www.menorcasailing.co.uk

Menorca Nautic
Moll de Llevant, 303 | Maó
Tel. 971 35 45 43 | www.menorcanautic.com
Barbarrossa Nautica Charter
Moll de Llevant, 230 | Maó
669 863 486 | www.barbarossanautica.com

BOAT RENTAL
The following companies also rent out boats (including motor boats)
and sometimes prepare a "charter" trip:
Antiga Meloussa
Moll de Ponent, 55 | Maó | 629 930 406 | www.menorcaenvelero.com
Fairline Menorca
Moll de Llevant, 186 | Maó | 971 35 51 01
www.fairlinemenorca.com
Nautic Fun
Marina Menorca | Maó | 971 36 42 50
www.nauticfunmenorca.com
Nàutica Reynés
Bajolí, 42 | POIMA | Maó | Tel. 971 36 24 84
www.nauticareynes.com
Servinautic
Pol. Ind. Llinaritx P-14 | Es Mercadal | Tel. 629 273 209
www.servinauticmenorca.com
Catamarán Charter
Passeig Marítim, 69 | Fornells | Tel. 626 48 64 26
www.catamarancharter.net
Nàutica Tecnimar S.L.
c/ Sabaters, 35 | POICI | Ciutadella | Tel. 971 38 05 38
www.nauticatecnimar.com
Menorcaboats
c/ Marina, 78 | Port de Ciutadella | Tel. 971 48 42 81
www.menorcaboats.com
Pons i Faner
Port de Cala en Bosc | Ciutadella | Tel. 610 26 12 91
www.barcosdealquiler.com
Catamarán Ocean Cat
Port de Ciutadella | Ciutadella | Tel. 680 729 138
http://velerooceancatciutadella.blogspot.com.es

NAUTICAL INSTALLATIONS

Maó Port Authority
Tel. 971 36 30 66
www.puertomao.com
Club Marítim de Maó
Tel. 971 36 50 22
www.clubmaritimomahon.com
Marina Mahón
Moll de Llevant 305
Tel. 971 36 67 87
www.marinamahon.es
Marina de Menorca (Maó)
Tel. 971 36 58 89
www.marinamenorca.com
Club Nàutic des Castell
Tel. 971 36 58 84
clubnauticovillacarlos.blogspot.com.es
Port d'Addaia
Tel. 971 35 86 49
www.puertoaddaya.com
Port de Fornells
Tel. 971 37 66 04
www.portsib.es
Club Nàutic de Fornells
Tel. 971 37 63 28
www.cnfornells.com
Port de Ciutadella
Tel. 971 48 44 55
www.portsib.es
Club Nàutic de Ciutadella
Tel. 971 38 39 18
www.cnciutadella.com
Puerto Deportivo Cala en Bosc
Tel. 971 38 71 71
www.portsib.es
Club Nàutic S'Algar
Tel. 971 36 07 00

DIVING

Dive Inn Menorca
Pla de Sant Joan, 10 | Port de Ciutadella
Tel. 651 644 319 | www.diveinnmenorca.com

Centro de Buceo Poseidón
Cala Santandria | Ciutadella
Tel. 971 38 26 44
www.bahia-poseidon.de

Bluewater Scuba
Cala en Bosc | Ciutadella
Tel. 971 38 71 83
www.bluewaterscuba.co.uk

Sub Menorca
c/ de la Platja | Cala en Bosc | Ciutadella
Tél. 609 656 916 | www.submenorca.info

Galdana Diving Centre
Hotel Los Gavilanes | Cala Galdana
Ferreries | Tel. 971 15 45 45
www.infotelecom.es/diving-galdana

Fornells Diving Center
Passeig Marítim, 68 | Fornells
Tel. 971 37 64 31
www.divingfornells.com

Diving Menorca
Hotel Carema Club Playa | Platges de Fornells
Tel. 625 712 631
www.divingmenorca.com

Triton Diving Center
Cala Torret | Local 3 | Sant Lluís
Tel. 617 685 193
www.tritondivingcenter.com

S'Algar Diving
S'Algar | Sant Lluís
Tel. 971 15 06 01
www.salgardiving.com

Scuba Plus
Ed. Las Terrazas | Cala en Busquets
Tel. 696 903 160
www.scubaplus.org

Deep-sea diving provides its fans with a wide range of hidden scenery

CYCLE-TOURING

Bicycle lovers have discovered the suitability of this means of transport when getting to know the island in more detail and, in particular, the inland scenery. The **Lighthouse Route** (Ruta dels Fars) and the **International Tour of Menorca** (Volta Internacional a Menorca)*, which has been held since 2001, are events with growing success among local and foreign participants. The presence of cyclists on the roads has increased as a result of these events, but the multiplying effect goes beyond that: on many tracks one sees well-equipped mountain bike riders pass by wearing their helmet, with increasing frequency and in greater numbers, which has led to the existence of a high participation **mountain bike Volta a Menorca****.

From a growing demand, the different councils are introducing bike lanes in distinct sections of their roadways, and there are now seven well-signposted routes that we detail below.

The routes are one way and are always between two towns:

1 Ciutadella-Ferreries	17.9 km	2 h (approx.)
2 Ferreries-Es Mercadal	14.6 km	1 h 45 m (approx.)
3 Es Mercadal-Alaior	7.3 km	45 m (approx.)

BICYCLE RENTAL

MAÓ

Ciclos Tramontana
Camí des Castell, 241C
Tel. 971 35 39 23
www.ciclostramontana.com

Menorsur
Moll de Llevant, 35
Tel. 971 36 15 00
www.autosmenorsur.com

Velo Rent Bike
c/ Francesc Femenies, 44
Tel. 971 35 37 98
www.bikemenorca.com

CIUTADELLA

Motos Peralta
c/ Sant Antoni, 62
Tel. 971 38 24 66

Tot Velo
c/ Eivissa, 59
Tel. 971 48 11 48
www.totvelo.com

Velos Joan
c/ Sant Isidre, 32
Tel. 971 38 15 76
www.velosjoan.com

FORNELLS

Dia Complert
(see p. 246, trekking)

SANT LLUÍS

Autos Valls
c/ Mestral, 2
(Platja de Punta Prima)
Tel. 971 15 90 00
www.autosvalls.com

4 Alaior-Maó	12.2 km	1 h 15 m (approx.)
5 Maó-Es Castell	8.4 km	45 m (approx.)
6 Es Castell-Sant Lluís	6.3 km	35 m (approx.)
7 Sant Lluís-Punta Prima	5.3 km	30 m (approx.)

Nearly all of them are classified as low difficulty routes, which mean they are suitable for beginners, with the exception of number 2, considered to be of medium difficulty. As some sections go along tracks without asphalt, it is recommended to ride mountain bikes.

Of course the best time for going cycle-touring is in spring and autumn, when the roads are far less busy than in summer and one does not need to add the high temperatures to the effort made in pedalling. It is quite possible that if the development of cycling continues in its progression, the seasonal nature of tourism will soon be broken by the impetus of these cycling fans.

* They are events organised by the **Cycle-touring Association of Menorca** (Moll de Llevant, number 173, in Port de Maó, tel 971 36 48 16 | www.ciclomenorca.com)
Organised by the **Penya Ciclista Ciutadella (c/ Eivissa, 10. Tel. 630 452 745 www.penyaciclistaciutadella.com)

An increasingly common scene on the roads of the island

OTHER ACTIVITIES

In summer, the sea is the most common setting for leisure activities, but there are other possibilities for doing exercise. The eight districts each have their own sports centre, the majority of which have tennis courts and in Maó, Es Mercadal and Ciutadella, swimming pools too. Grouped by activity, the following addresses may be of interest:

TREKKING
Dia Complert
Excursions and adventure.
Passeig Marítim, 41. Fornells.
Tel. 609 67 09 96 | www.diacomplert.com
Menorca en Kayak
Kayak excursions. S'Arribada, 8. Es Grau.
Tel. 669 09 79 77 | www.menorcaenkayak.com
Rutas Menorca
Guided walkings. c/ Verge del Toro, 10.
Es Mercadal. Tel. 685 74 73 08
www.rutasmenorca.com

GOLF
Club Son Parc
Urbanización Son Parc. Es Mercadal.
Tel. 971 18 88 75 | www.golfsonparc.com

HORSE RIDING
The great love of horses goes well beyond the setting of the festivals. There are classical dressage schools and trotting races are regularly held in the **Municipal Hippodrome** of Maó and the **Torre des Ram** in Ciutadella (www.hipodromdemao.com). In summer, the **Ganadería son Martorellet** de Ferreries (Cala Galdana road), performs an equestrian show on Tuesdays and Thursdays (from 8.30 p.m. onwards).
Tel. 639 15 68 51 www.sonmartorellet.com

They offer other services related to horse-riding as do the following centres:

Cavalls Son Angel Camí d'Algaiarens, Ciutadella. Tel. 609 83 39 02 | www.cavallssonangel.com
Centre Eqüestre Equimar Camí Verd, parc. 84, Maó. Tel. 669 255 487.
Club Hípic Alaior Es Cós. Tel. 670 34 39 75.
Club Hípic Ciutadella Camí des Caragol.
Tel. 971 09 15 10 | www.clubhipicciutadella.com
Club Hípic Maó Road Maó-Ciutadella km 4 near Talatí turning at rigth. Tel. 626 08 43 52 www.clubhipicmao.com
Club Hípic Sa Creueta Camí de la Figuerenya, 18, Es Migjorn Gran. Tel. 616 95 36 36. www.sacreueta.com
Club Hípic Ses Ramones c/ Hort des jurats. Es Mercadal. Tel. 676 81 89 00.

Horse riding schools:
Escola Eqüestre Menorquina Camí des Caragol, 44, Ciutadella. Tel. 607 49 68 24 www.escolaequestremenorquina.es
Grup Cavallers Quadres Bintaufa c/ Cós de Gràcia, 56, Maó. Tel. 670 21 42 92.
Menorca a Cavall Lloc de Santa Rita, road Es Mercadal-Ferreries. Tel. 626 59 37 37 www.menorcaacavall.com

RESERVA DE LA CONCEPCIÓ
The *Concepció* reserve is a sustaianable tourist project located in the bay of Fornells. They organise volunteer days hand-collecting sea salt in exchange for bed and breakfast in their installations. Tel. 971 05 40 45
http://lareservadelaconcepcio.wordpress.com

ACCOMMODATION

Hotels on the island are generally found in the coastal developments alongside the beaches, and it is to where the majority of tourists flock. The list of hotels, including both hotels and apartments, would take up more space than this entire guide and is available to anyone interested from the tourist offices. In contrast, we thought it would be interesting to point out those that have recently opened within the framework of "green" tourism and off the beaten track and which are in line with the desired sustainable growth guidelines.

AGROTOURISM

As well as accommodation they generally provide breakfast, with local produce and will soon provide the possibility of organising lunches and suppers to order (www.menorcaturismorural.net).

Alcaufar Vell Sant Lluís, (21 rooms). Road to Alcalfar, km 8.
Tel. 971 15 18 74 | www.alcaufarvell.com

Atalis Es Migjorn Gran. At the end of Sant Tomàs urbanization.
Tel. 971 37 04 61 | www.fincaatalis.com

Biniatram Ciutadella, (8 rooms). Swimming pool, tennis court, garden.
Road to Cala Morell, km 7. Tel. 971 38 31 13 | www.biniatram.com

Binisaid Ferreries, (6 rooms). Swimming pool, petanque. Road to Cala Galdana. km 4.3. Tel. 971 15 50 63 | www.binisaid.com

Ca Na Xini Ferreries, (5 rooms). Camí de Sant Patrici, s/n.
Tel. 971 37 45 12 | www.canaxini.com

Llucmaçanes Gran Maó, (7 rooms). Pla de Sant Gaietà, 10.
Tel. 971 35 21 17 | www.llucmagran.com

Matxaní Gran Maó, (10 rooms). Road to Sant Climent–Binidalí km. 1.5
Tel. 971 15 33 37 | www.matxani-gran.com

Sant Joan de Binissaida Es Castell, (12 rooms). Camí de Binissaida, 108.
Tel. 971 35 55 98 | www.binissaida.com

Lloc de Sant Tomàs Ciutadella, (4 rooms). Horse-ridings.
Camí Vell, km 3. Tel. 646 278 537

Sa Torre Blanca Maó, Road Maó-Fornells, Camí de sa Boval.
Tel. 971 18 83 08 | www.satorreblanca.com

Son Triay Nou Ferreries, (8 rooms). Swimming pool, tennis court, garden. Road to Cala Galdana. km 2.5.
Tel. 971 15 50 78 | www.sontriay.com

Turmaden des capità Alaior, (4 rooms). Swimming pool, garden.
Road to Es Migjorn. km 1. Tel. 971 37 80 65 | www.turmaden.com

COUNTRY HOTELS

Biniarroca Sant Lluís, (18 rooms). Camí de Biniarroca, 57.
Tel. 971 15 00 59 | www.biniarroca.com

Binigaus Vell Es Migjorn, (20 rooms). Camí de sa mala garba, km 0.9
Tel. 971 05 07 22 | www.binigausvell.com

Binissafullet Vell Sant Lluís, (8 rooms). Road to Binissafúller, 64.
Tel. 971 15 66 33 | www.binissafullet.com

Morvedrà Nou Ciutadella, (17 rooms). Camí de St. Joan de Missa, 7.
Tel. 971 35 95 21 | www.morvedranou.es
Sant Ignasi Ciutadella, (25 rooms). Turning off the road to Cala
Morell. Tel. 971 38 55 75 | www.santignasi.com
Son Granot Es Castell, (8 rooms). Road Sant Felip s/n.
Tel. 971 35 55 55 | www.songranot.com
Torralbenc Alaior, (22 rooms). Road Maó-Cala'n Porter, km 10.
Tel. 971 37 72 11 | www.torralbenc.com

INLAND TOURISM

This category is different from the above in that the houses concerned
have been absorbed in time by the urban centres of the towns.
Casa Albertí Maó, (6 rooms), c/ Isabel II, 9.
Tel. 971 35 42 10 | www.casalberti.com
Ses Sucreres Ferreries, (6 rooms), c/ Sant Joan, 15.
Tel. 971 37 41 92 | www.hotelsessucreres.com
Son Tretze Sant Lluís, (8 rooms/16 beds). Camí de Binifadet, 20.
It possesses a large multi-purpose room.
Tel. 971 15 09 43 | www.sontretze.com
Hotel Tres Sants Ciutadella, (8 rooms). C. Sant Cristòfol, 2.
Tel. 971 48 22 08 | www.hoteltressants.com

CAMPSITES, HOSTELS AND SUMMER CAMP HOUSES

Camping Son Bou Alaior. Sant Jaume road, km 3.5. Pleasant setting
and fine views. Bungalows, wooden cabins, swimming pool, restau-
rant, supermarket. Tel. 971 37 27 27 | www.campingsonbou.com
Camping S'Atalaia Ferreries. Road to Cala Galdana, km 4. Surrounded
by pine forest, with swimming pool, restaurant, supermarket and
other services. Tel. 971 37 42 32 | www.campingsatalaia.com
  Besides those already mentioned and those providing the traditional type of stay, there are, though not very many, other alternative
establishments providing accommodation particularly for groups
interested in an educational visit. **Binixems** Alaior. with bunk beds
and basic facilities, attached to the hermitage and **Son Putxet**, with
two equipped houses and a camping area. Tel. 971 37 11 07.
Binitalaiot Ciutadella. Summer camp house. Tel. 971 38 37 00
Es Pinaret Ciutadella. Well equipped hostel, and camping area.
Tel. 971 38 10 50
Sant Joan de Missa. Ciutadella. Attached to the hermitage of the
same name, it has good facilities. Tel. 971 38 10 82

Es Torretó Ciutadella. Summer camp house. Tel. 971 36 50 73
Sa Vinyeta Ciutadella. Hostel. Tel. 971 48 77 63
Santa Eularieta Alaior, Camí d'en Kane. Tel. 971 36 50 73
Sanctuary of El Toro Es Mercadal. Symbolic spot, making use of the space offered by the monastic cells. Tel. 971 37 50 60
Es Canaló Ferreries. At the start of the Algendar ravine.
Tel. 971 37 40 72
Biniparratx campsite Sant Lluís. With house-refuge and wild camping.
Tel. 971 36 50 73
Es Pinaret de s'Algar Sant Lluís. Camping area with drinking water, tables and wooden benches. Tel. 971 15 09 50

The rural accommodations makes possible to live the day-to-day of the Menorcan countryside

TRANSPORT

AIR

The companies that run scheduled flights throughout the year from Barcelona, Palma de Mallorca, Madrid and Valencia are:

Air Europa +34 902 40 15 01 | www.aireuropa.com
Iberia +34 902 40 05 00 | www.iberia.es
Ryanair +44 871 246 0011 | www.ryanair.com
Vueling +34 807 20 01 00 | www.vueling.com

There are more flights on offer at Easter and in the summer, when several airlines run flights between the island and distinct European capitals. The airport is situated on the Me-14 road, between Maó and Sant Climent.

Airport 971 15 70 00 | www.aena.es

BOAT

In winter the **Acciona-Trasmediterránea** company runs a service between Maó and Barcelona with three trips per week. This route becomes daily at Easter and during the summer months, and is often backed up by a second boat during peak holiday periods. There are two types of boat: a fast one, covering the trip in four hours, and another one that does it in eight hours. Another regular route is Maó-Palma (about six hours journey), which continues on to Valencia, with a weekly service throughout the year.
Tel. 902 45 46 45 | www.trasmediterranea.es

Throughout the year **Baleària** makes trips daily to Barcelona, with a fast boat and a normal one, and one to Mallorca (fast).
Tel. 902 16 01 80 | www.balearia.com

Iscomar Covers the Ciutadella-Alcúdia route in a journey lasting three hours, twice a day. It is a good alternative for tourism between the islands using your own car.
Tel. 902 11 91 28 | www.iscomar.com

BUSES

There are three companies that run regular bus routes:
Transports Menorca S.A. Cover the Maó-Ciutadella, Maó-Es Castell, Maó-Sant Lluís, Maó-Es Migjorn Gran-Ferreries, Maó-Sant Climent

It is worth remembering that the speed limit between towns is 90 kph and 40 kph inside the towns. Moreover, on rural tracks it is advisable to sound the horn or flash the lights in order to warn of your presence before many curves, where visibility is limited. The scarcity of special bike lanes and wide pavements is another factor that makes it a good idea to drive slowly, along with the frequently changing gradients in the road. It is quite common to be detained on the secondary roads, at least for a few minutes, by small herds of cows on their way to or returning from their grazing land.

routes, and those round the urbanisations in the southeast area.
Tel. 971 36 04 75 | www.tmsa.es.
The bus station in Maó is in **S'Esplanada**.
Autos Fornells S.A. Link Maó with Fornells and the urbanised beach-
es on the northeast coast (Arenal d'en Castell, Son Parc, Platges de
Fornells and Es Grau).
Tel. 971 15 43 90 / 686 939 246 | www.autosfornells.com
Autocars Torres Links Ciutadella with the urbanised beaches around
the city (Cala Morell, Son Saura, Sa Caleta, Santandria, Cala Blanca,
Cala en Bosc, Son Xoriguer, Cala en Blanes, Los Delfines and Cala en
Forcat) and with the Son Blanc harbour. It also connects Maó with its
port and the airport. Tel. 971 38 47 20 | www.e-torres.net

We recommend you check the timetables in advance at the bus stations or in the tourist information offices since in winter the service
is greatly reduced. You can also check in the **Diari Menorca** (www.
menorca.info), which has a daily page, **Agenda**, where you will find
information times of planes, boats, buses, petrol stations, all night
chemists, cinemas and a culture guide.

CAR

There are international and local car hire firms in most of the towns.
The biggest ones have offices and pick-up and return services at the
airport. Remember that the demand increases greatly during the
peak holiday season and it is a good idea to book your vehicle in
advance. Travel agencies and airlines often provide plane-car and
boat-car packages that are more economical.

TAXIS

It is possible to get a taxi in the stands of the different towns.
Tel. 971 36 71 11 / 971 48 22 22 | www.taximenorca.es

Index of toponyms

ORGANISATIONS AND PUBLIC SERVICE

Menorca Island Council
Tel. 971 35 60 50
www.cime.es
Balear Islands Council
Tel. 971 17 65 65
Menorca Hoteliers Association
Tel. 902 110 111
www.visitmenorca.com
Fundació Destí (Information and promotion of tourism in Menorca)
Tel. 971 36 86 78 | www.menorca.es

TOURIST INFORMATION OFFICES
Maó
Pl. Constitució, Town Hall
Tel. 971 36 37 90
Ciutadella
Pl. des Born, Town Hall
Tel. 971 48 41 55
Aeroport
Tel. 971 15 71 15
Port de Maó
Moll de Llevant, 2
Tel. 971 35 59 52

CONSULATES
Great Britain Sa Casa Nova. Camí de Bini-trap, 30. Es Castell. Tel. 971 36 78 18
Germany Negres, 32. Maó. Tel. 971 36 16 68
France Av. Argentina 45A. Palma (Majorca)
Tel. 971 73 03 01
Italy Road Portopí 8. Palma (Majorca)
Tel. 971 40 56 68

TOWN COUNCILS
Maó Tel. 971 36 98 00
www.ajmao.org
Ciutadella Tel. 971 38 10 50
www.ajciutadella.org
Alaior Tel. 971 37 10 02
www.alaior.org
Es Mercadal Tel. 971 37 50 02
www.aj-esmercadal.org
Ferreries Tel. 971 37 30 03
www.ajferreries.org
Sant Lluís Tel. 971 15 09 50
www.ajsantlluis.org
Es Castell Tel. 971 36 51 93
www.aj-escastell.org
Es Migjorn Gran Tel. 971 37 01 10
www.ajmigjorngran.org

EMERGENCIES
(co-ordinating all the emergency services)
Tel. 112
National Police (emergencies)
Tel. 091
www.policia.es
Civil Guard
Tel. 062
www.guardiacivil.org
Sea rescue
Tel. 900 20 22 02
www.salvamentomaritimo.es
Weather information
Tel. 807 17 03 65
www.inm.es
Maritime weather information
Tel. 807 17 03 70
www.inm.es

Building of the Menorca Island Council in the Plaça de la Biosfera in Maó

The main beaches have Red Cross assistance services

HEALTHCARE AREA
http://portaldesalut.caib.es

Hospital Mateu Orfila
Ronda de Malbúger, 1
Maó
Tel. 971 48 70 00
www.ibsalut.es

Dalt Sant Joan Health Centre
c/ Fornells, 107
Maó
Tel. 971 35 32 55

Canal Salat Health Centre
c/ Sant Antoni M. Claret, s/n
Ciutadella
Tel. 971 48 01 12

Es Banyer Health Centre
c/ Mestre Duran, s/n
Alaior
Tel. 971 37 29 31

Mobile ICU
(Emergencies/Ambulances)
Tel. 061

Red Cross

Maó	971 36 11 80
Ciutadella	971 38 19 93
Alaior	971 37 12 38
Ferreries	971 37 31 39
Mercadal	971 15 41 98
Sant Lluís	971 15 10 01